Vivid

Vivid

Style in Colour

Words **Julia Green**
Photography **Armelle Habib**

Hardie Grant

BOOKS

CONTENTS

Introduction   7

Orange   11

Red   33

Blue   65

Green   95

Pink   133

Yellow   157

White   199

Black   235

Credits   260
Acknowledgements   261
About the authors   263

INTRODUCTION

Striking and beautiful rooms are often full of carefully considered colour – colour injects emotion into a space and arouses feelings in visitors and occupants alike. It is the clever contrast of colours that casts a spell on us long before we sink into a delicious armchair or notice the view.

Colour is one of the most exciting components of a home's interior. It can set the mood, be used for its decorative beauty or be an entirely creative outlet for decorators who recognise its power.

In interior design, colour is a visual language that allows you to stamp your own style onto your surrounds by adding, editing or combining items in your space in expressive, maybe even daring, ways.

If you've ever entered a space – perhaps even your own – and thought it looked nondescript or felt unfinished, it's most likely that the colour choices for paint and decorative elements were safe ones. What will lift that room is masterful use of colour.

This book is about bringing colour into the home. During lockdowns around the world, we've had time to scrutinise our surroundings, reflect and, sometimes, longingly seek inspiration elsewhere, and in many cases have found our own nests drab indeed. With our focus on home, in this book we pay some serious attention to those who have carried off interior colour with aplomb, dissect why it works and help you follow suit.

I grew up surrounded by a kaleidoscope of colour. My mother embraced the rainbow with vigour in my childhood home, and the influences of the disco era were evident in her decorating, which buzzed with vibrant fuchsias and glittery silvers. I trace my fearless approach to colour back to that creative atmosphere and sense of freedom – my love for contrasting colours began there.

My sense of colour appreciation evolved as I moved through life. Travels in my twenties took me overseas, to exotic destinations where tradition and colour were stunningly intertwined. Morocco still captivates me with its rich and varied palette. Likewise, the reds, golds and olive greens of Tuscany warm my heart, and I'm grounded by the more muted colours of the Australian native landscape: I continue to find inspiration everywhere.

Colour has always felt like a language I can converse in, and it is a medium I feel in touch with from an emotional perspective. From my

amateur beginnings as a stylist to making a career of it, my confidence with colour has been my trademark for more than a decade.

I've been privileged to work with design teams all around Australia, staging and styling photoshoots for clients, magazines, TV and brands, and I was lucky to often be paired with talented photographer Armelle Habib. Now my friend and collaborator, Armelle shares my passion for colour and this has been captured to stunning effect throughout this book, thanks to her exceptional eye.

Styling is all about changing the complexion of a room without structural work. My passion is choreographing colour, through fabrics, furniture, decorative finishes, accessories and artwork. You may have hit an inspirational wall when it comes to your own home – we aim here to guide you through a new way of thinking about colour, through a visual display of it at work.

Nowadays, thanks to far-reaching TV programs and magazines, social media, style expos and influencers, use of colour in our personal spaces is no longer the domain of designers alone. People are more comfortable experimenting in their homes to change its look. I suggest you begin by looking dispassionately and critically at what you've got already: the bones are likely there. The good news is that a design refresh, or even a bolder overhaul, does not have to be a huge financial commitment or a once-in-a-decade event. Your home may just need a small touch-up in one room or two to make it sing.

I understand there is an element of nervousness for some when it comes to selecting colour for their lives and their homes. For a few, that fear is real and an entirely black or navy wardrobe prevails, or every surface at home is a monochrome white. Whenever I have confronted such fears in others, the root cause is the same: anxiety about making the wrong choice.

Vivid is dedicated to those who have ignored the notion of wrong choices and have gone with their gut instincts instead. We are celebrating their bravery and colour confidence. We also want to encourage more people to follow suit!

The approach we have taken is to take a close look at eight key colours and show you how they can work in today's interiors. I touch on colour psychology and take you inside a selection of diverse interiors, from all over the world, where colour is used with confidence. This is no technical manual on colour theory, but a portfolio of inspiration looking at interiors created with flair, style and commitment to colour.

Essays and interviews offer further insight into working with different hues. Each chapter features dozens of Armelle's stunning photographs – detail, texture and tone: a tempting colour swatch in itself. Together, we hope this richly illustrated guide will act as part mood board, part catalogue, to kickstart your own implementation at home.

Armelle and I hope this book inspires you to experiment with colour. We hope it stimulates creativity and motivates you to create your own vivid sanctuary.

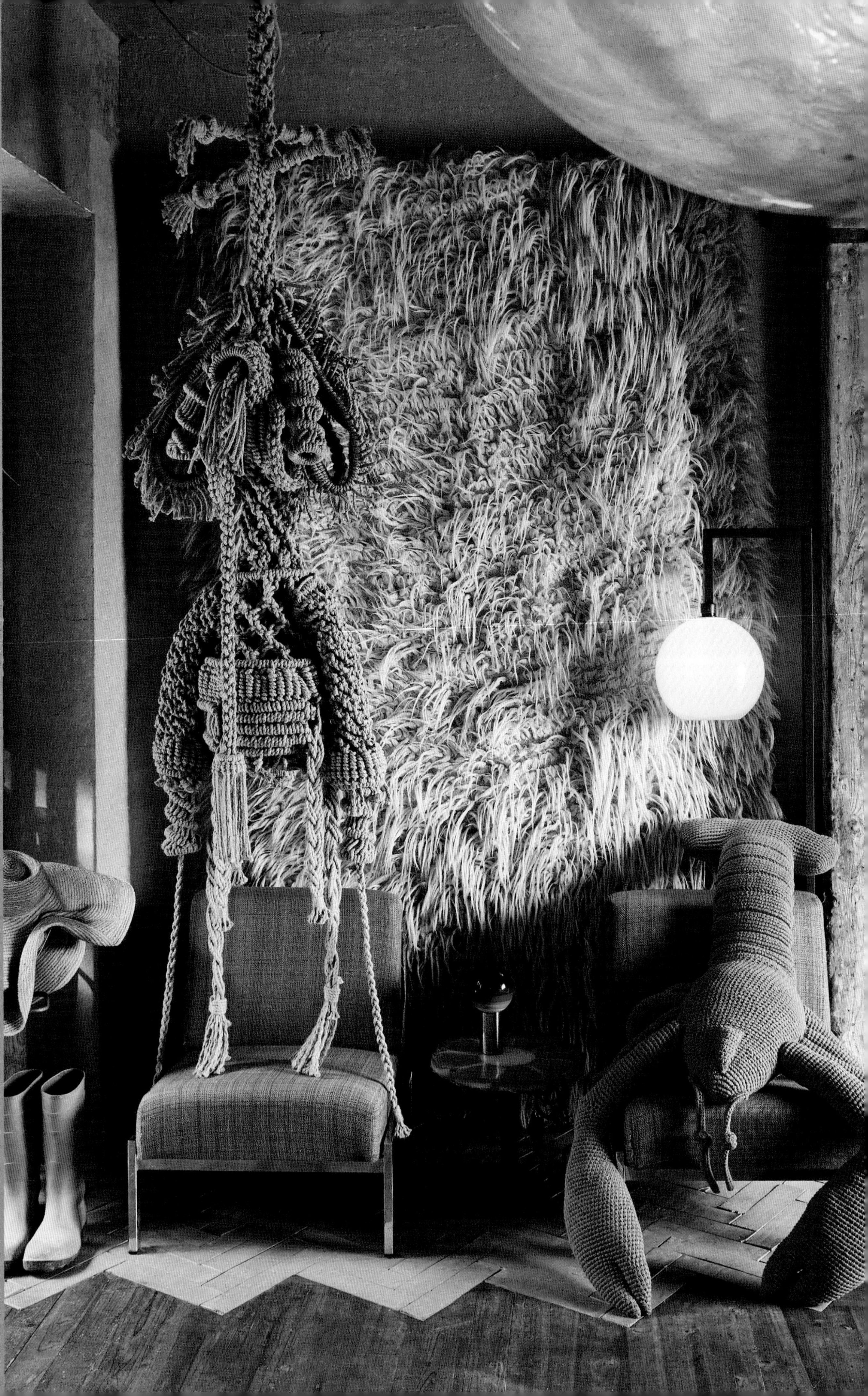

Sunny but earthy orange is a gorgeous accent colour – just think of the tints found in pumpkin, bronze, peach, brass and flame. For me, the colour orange conjures warmth, like the dipping glow of a sunset, and when I see it used in interiors, I think of the zesty, punchy flavour of its namesake sun-ripened fruit.

From piquant marmalade to fresh papaya and earthy clay, orange feels restorative too, like it could fix a cold, and adds a joyful note to interiors that embrace it. Although it sits in the warmer spectrum of colour, it can be used in the home across all four seasons to full advantage. A couple of bright mango market umbrellas in the courtyard or on the deck sing of summer, yet a textured persimmon wool throw is a cosy beacon in winter. While close to a 'hot' colour, it is not as aggressive as red – perhaps consider it a spice.

Orange is fresh, optimistic and exudes happiness. It is encouraging, extroverted and doesn't mind showing off. Orange is energetic, but can be mellowed when combined with softer hues such as lilac – in fact, that pairing is one of my all-time favourites.

Given its eye-catching nature, it is not surprising to see orange often used as a colour in advertising; in the home, people can be a little afraid to use it due to this same intensity.

My advice is to gently introduce orange into your world as an accent. This will determine if you are able to live with it harmoniously, and if it troubles you or takes too much of your attention, it is easy to remove.

Even a little bit of orange can have a big impact. A melon armchair, for example, can be a statement piece in a room. Reflect the bold hue in artwork or smaller decorative items to allow it to really come alive.

In a bedroom setting, a coral throw or cushions can bring a fresh burst of colour against crisp white bed linen. Likewise, ceramics or glassware can reference hues that perhaps feature in nearby art, bringing a hint of colour and adding understated interest – orange doesn't have to be full strength. It works well in geometric prints, with textured fabrics like corduroy and velvet, chunky weaves and against most natural materials.

Kitchens, too, are spaces where orange can really work – and not just in retro-inspired spaces. A pop of tangerine in a contemporary kitchen, for example in pendant lighting, can provide a fun and confident modern touch.

Set against white, orange is bold and fresh, but it works harmoniously when tempered with greys and timber tones, too.

Orange

← Gradations of the same colour, in different shades and intensities, provide maximum impact in this space, rather than an overwhelming use of one shade. Try creating an ombre effect for visual interest.

← Texture plays a key role with accent colours. By using a mixture of materials for your decorative items, the eye is attracted to both texture and colour. This way, you can warm up a space for the winter months with shaggy wools, or keep it cool for summer with breezy linens.

↑ Autumn colours add a golden glow to a space, whether using real or crafted foliage and flowers. For a dramatic effect, think big: opt for large pots or branch-like installations that are in proportion to the height and scale of a space. A large, loose arrangement creates a relaxed vibe here.

↑ To highlight the use of one colour you do not need to saturate a space with it. In fact, a small hint of it, like a light piece of flowing fabric as the standout hue, can have plenty of subtle impact.

→ Pair bold orange with natural materials such as rattan to soften a space.

Stripes demand your attention. Try reupholstering chairs with a stripe in your favourite accent colour, drawn from the same palette as wall, floor or ceiling colours.

→ Lighting with a soft, ambient glow will warm a space, especially in a room with hard finishes. A cool light used in a concrete space will give it a lab-like effect. Carefully select the bulb for its wattage and its role in the space: warm light casts a yellowish tint.

Gold-coloured accessories, such as gilded mirrors and tapware, are an effective and unconventional way to introduce subtle orange hues, as are warm, golden-coppery tones in decorative items.

Rozemarijn de Witte
and Pierre Traversier

Los Enamorados, Ibiza, Spain

Tell us a little about creating this space. What was it inspired by?

The inspiration for the hotel came from many things. We always make old-school collages before beginning an interior, to create a clear starting point. Most important was that we wanted to create something imaginative, but at the same time laid-back and relaxed. Since we travel a lot ourselves, we had a strong idea about how it needed to feel. It needed to be beautiful, colourful, comfortable, with a certain luxury, without being cold or snobbish. All lights needed to be dimmable, beds needed to be the best you've ever felt. You can choose a duvet or only a linen sheet to sleep under. You can sleep with the doors of your balcony open to the sound of the sea and still make the room completely dark.

We wanted to design a hotel where guests feel completely at home; where you travel when you stay put.

Have you always loved colour?

Yes. Almost everything in Ibiza is white and we wanted to do something completely opposite. Nothing in the hotel is white except for the toilet and the toilet paper.

We love to mix colour and find unexpected combinations. Every room has different-coloured tiles, paint, furniture, yet the atmosphere in each room is alike. The rooms are like sisters: different, but they get along well.

How has your style evolved over the years?

Things evolve always; you have seen more, you have learned more. But at its base it stays the same. We love to mix vintage with design, rough with soft, old with new, pale with bright.

To us, it is important that you work with what you have, with respect for what is already there. For example, we removed the fake marble tiles and replaced them with original Spanish terracotta tiles; we changed the white wall paint and enhanced the rough concrete structure that was underneath. We kept the layout of the hotel, but changed the atmosphere. Keep what is great, add what is better.

Do you have a favourite colour, pattern or similar that you often turn to?

My favourite colour is orange. It is sunny and represents happiness for me, so I do like to use orange where I can. We live in different places and countries, and the colours we use are always different.

I like dark colours very much too. In Amsterdam, we live on an old iron houseboat, and the atmosphere there is dark and moody. I don't feel that bright colours work there. Although he knows it is not a colour, Pierre's favourite colour is black.

We have slightly different tastes but we can always find something that we both like – mixing things up is quite natural.

How do you incorporate colour into your home?

We always start with what kind of place we have and where it is situated. Our finca in Ibiza is light and bright; it is painted an off white combined with coloured carpets and a mix of rattan and more modern furniture. The house in Paris is much darker; the walls are in all different shades of green and browns, but with brighter colours in design and vintage furniture.

Do you have a favourite item within your hotel?

Pierre's favourite item is the dolphin-tail chair, bought from an artist on the island. Mine is the orange Panton hanging lamp and the concrete structures of Jonathan Adler, now located next to the reception – who knows where they will be next season, because we change the decor every year to keep it fresh, to always have a surprise for regular guests and for our own enjoyment.

How does colour influence the way you live?
In every way. I am quite a perfectionist and I love it when things go well together: I will never wear black underwear under a pink dress, or nude under a black dress! So even when you don't see it, I want it to match. That means that I drive everybody crazy, including those who work behind the scenes in the bar, kitchen and in maintenance. Why sweep the floor with a metal and blue plastic broom when you can find an orange or wicker one that makes you happy?

Who or what inspires you?
I am a visual and intuitive person, so I gain inspiration everywhere and from all my senses. Travel, smells, smiles; magazines, stores, hotels. Nature, sunset, stars; flowers, food, fountains. Inspiration is everywhere.

The creative challenge is never to copy but to combine things you have seen, heard or felt in a new way. So that it becomes yours. I believe in authenticity. Always put your own personality into everything you do. Don't get hung up on what other people might think or like, do exactly what you think is nice. I love it when people dare to express themselves in everything they do, including how they dress. I can always appreciate a style, perhaps even more so when it is the opposite of mine. Otherwise the world would be boring.

The list of people that inspire me is long. From Jonathan Adler to Bas Kosters, Fong Leng to Audrey Hepburn. From Pippi Longstocking to Gaudi, Martin Luther King to Lucille Ball.

Do you have a favourite location or place to visit and why?
Yes, Japan, although the Japanese style of less is more is quite the opposite of ours. We really admire everything in Japan: the cleanness, the simplicity, the ceramics, food and elegance. We love their sense of harmony, the way they present things, pack things, create things. It's beautiful and inspirational.

THE PSYCHOLOGY OF COLOUR

While we all have our favourite colours, have you ever stopped to consider what draws you to certain shades?

Oscar Wilde summed it up perfectly when he said: 'Mere colour can speak to the soul in a thousand different ways'. Yet, we'd be hard pressed to explain how or why it does. But you know the feeling – when you've been stopped in your tracks by a display of colour in nature, a precise shade of an item, or a particular combination of colours that evokes a hard-to-articulate sensation.

As a colour lover in the strongest sense, it is the boldest, brightest hues that win my heart and prompt the strongest emotional response. But over time, I have learned to tune in to the psychology of different colours: I know that when creativity is calling me, yellow is the colour to surround myself with; or, if I am feeling melancholy, I will look to the moody hues of navy and indigo.

Here, we look at the associations we make in relation to some of our favourite colours, their symbolism, and how they might foster a particular mood or atmosphere.

TICKLED PINK

Pink represents romance, flowers and femininity, and it symbolises hope and awareness. Variations of pink can range from calming to stimulating. Bright pink can add energy and foster creativity, while a toned-down palette of pale pink can be soothing.

GOING GREEN

The palette of green is peaceful on the eye. It creates feelings of harmony, balance and positivity while at the same time renewing and restoring depleted energies. It is synonymous with life and new beginnings.

MELLOW YELLOW

Yellow is a wise colour choice for a study or for other learning environments thanks to its ability to support clarity of thought. As one of the more uplifting colours of the spectrum, it shines with hope, happiness and fun, yet also awakens creativity, optimism and enthusiasm.

INTO THE BLUE

Blue, in its many and varied shades, delivers a breath of fresh air. Mid-blue brings contentment, calmness and peace to interiors, while darker shades are synonymous with power and authority.

RED HOT

Red is strong-willed, powerful and energetic. This alpha colour symbolises confidence, creates excitement and is associated with determination. Due to its intensity, red is best used with restraint – in certain applications, it signifies danger.

PURPLE PATCH

No other colour seems to polarise like purple. But whatever your take, it is thought to encourage and support an innovative and creative mind. A shade that lends itself to minimalist settings, purple is a touch mystical and stimulates dream activity.

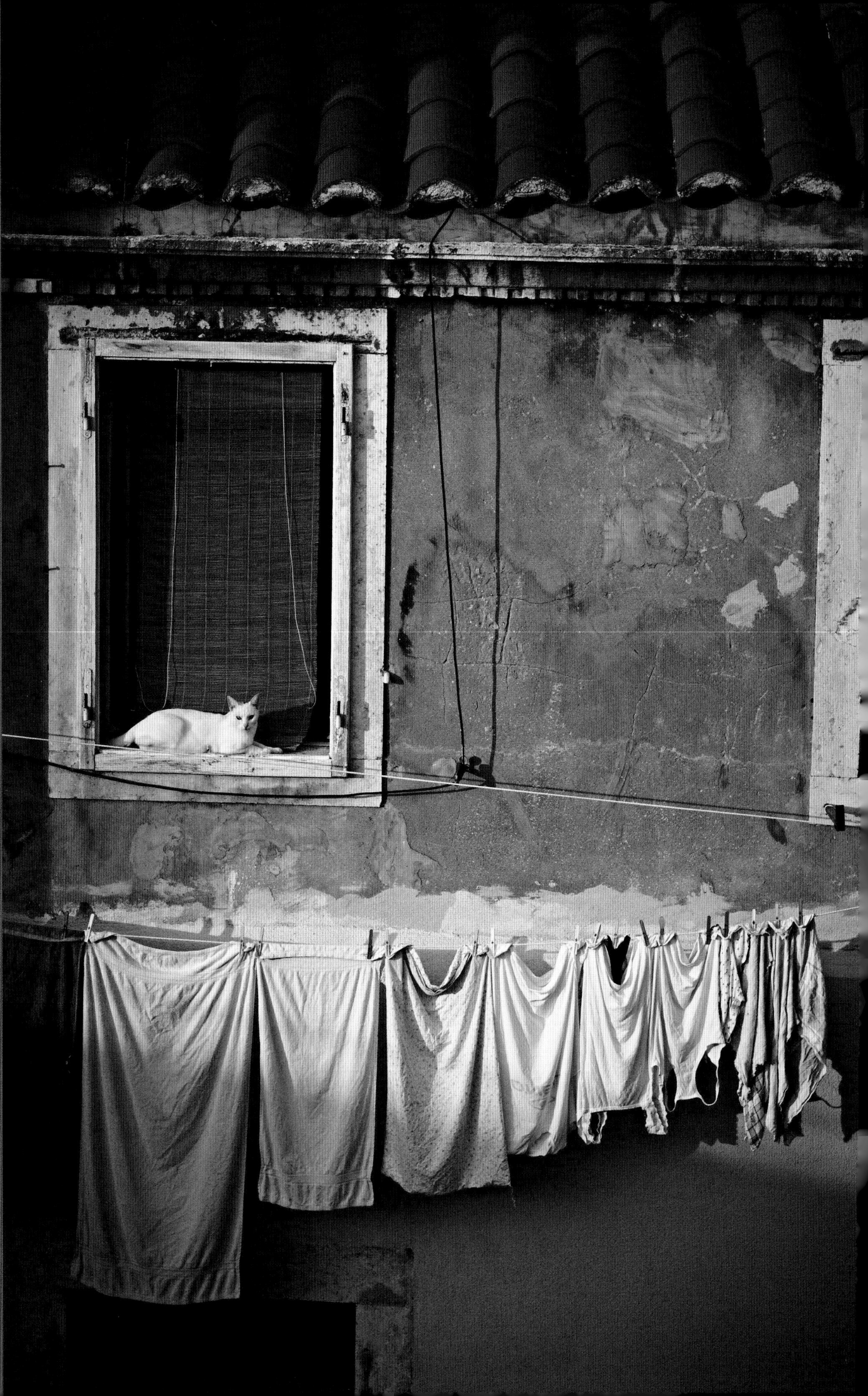

Red in all its incarnations – from deep jewel ruby tones to rust, gorgeous maroons and rustic terracotta – remains a classic and enduring favourite in interiors. And, when used well, it's easy to see why.

But use of such a powerful colour inside a home calls for caution. Overdoing red can, rather than creating warmth, feel clinical or border on aggressive. The secret to using red in interiors is moderation.

Statement pieces, such as an armchair in a rich ruby velvet or a sofa that draws on the more earthy tones of rust or a burnt red, will unequivocally incorporate red as a key colour in a bedroom or living room setting.

Consider adding shelves in a deep oxblood red, with a similar shade picked up in cushions contrasted with the snap of white trim or stripe. Choose natural materials as a neutral partner, such as sisal or rattan, weathered timber or oxidised metallics.

While it's not a colour I see widely used at full saturation, a standout interior I've come across teamed a bright red table lamp with a soft powder blue wall for a complete contrast. This bold statement lamp was then further tied into the interior with red accents in the feature artwork, completing the picture without dominating.

Consider blush pink as a colour foil, with deeper berry tones complementing red's vigour. Use incarnations of the primary hue in soft furnishings such as cushions or throw rugs, art, or even walls.

Likewise, cooler tones work when juxtaposed with scarlet. Shades of blue or teal are gorgeous complementary accent colours to counteract a warmer palette, while a cool grey will serve as an excellent background and still allow the feature shade to shine. Painting walls in an inconspicuous shade of light grey is another way to allow cherry-red pieces to sing without overpowering a room.

Jewel or earthy reds are the easiest to work with, but if it's a true candy-apple colour you love, consider tempering it by using it alongside natural elements. Try layering red with timber, for example: red dining chairs paired with a timber dining table sets an inviting, not confronting, tone.

Red

Layering varying shades of red – from maroon and magenta to cherry and rose – tempers a dominant colour and renders it playful. The soft pink wall is a successful colour foil in this informal red room.

↑ Rather than overwhelm, a flash of colour via understated accessories adds contrast and warmth to neutral tones and hard surfaces.

→ Linking rooms with colour gives a home a harmonious, deliberate look. By referencing the same colour, particularly in an open-plan space, the eye is drawn from one zone to the next, creating flow and visual continuity. Rust-coloured accents dotted around complete the colour jigsaw.

One of the secrets to using bold colours in interiors is moderation: restrained use of accent colours, both in volume and variety, makes a sophisticated statement.

While moderation is often necessary to achieve a desired look, in some cases, the same can be said of abundance. Layer a room with different tones of your chosen colour, varying the intensity and shade of the same hue. Layer with pattern as well as colour. Pattern-on-pattern requires confidence and a firm commitment – otherwise, it can look half-hearted.

→ Earthy tones have given rise to a resurgence of red in interior spaces, and while more often associated with cosiness, such colours are certainly not out of place in more minimalist, contemporary spaces. An understated space is given an element of warmth thanks to the inclusion of a rich amber couch, taking the room from stark to sophisticated.

→→ Balance is fundamental in a colour scheme. When planning your own palette, if warmer colours dominate, incorporate a cool shade for balance. Conversely, add a warming shade to an otherwise cool palette to avoid it feeling clinical.

A brick-red orb with an emerging grey graphic is striking on this cafe wall, balancing the pattern and strength of the black-and-white flooring. This shot of accent colour is a clear focal point, just as it would be on a more common monochrome backdrop.

Jessica Bettenay

Euroa, Australia

Tell us a little about creating this space. What was it inspired by?

I don't follow any set of rules or have a set style. For my design studio, Resident Avenue, style is influenced by two things: the space itself and the client that lives there.

This striking rural Victorian property takes inspiration from Ned Kelly's infamous last stand and our clients' love for the dramatic hilly landscape. This home is heavily design driven by the landscape and the desire to bring the outdoors in. A refined palette was used, but with interest added through layering textures and playing with colours that mimic seasonal changes. Lots of the detail of the property was about raw, natural and textural materials finding their way inside.

Have you always loved colour?

Always, although I have generally gravitated to unusual colours – colours that have a dirty, muddy and earthy base. When I was younger, all I ever wanted to wear was mustard-coloured clothes. I still love mustard and any colour that is reminiscent of nature and the landscape: dusty pinks, rust tones, yellow-based army greens, inky blues and deep maroons. I love blending colour combinations and textures in compelling and unexpected ways. For me, texture and colour go hand in hand. Used well, they add depth, interest and character to any space. Colour is integral to creating an interior that tells your story, reflects your journey through life.

The colours of the landscape were particularly relevant in the design development of this home. The colour in the kitchen came from the striking combinations of tones you see on the rocks through the huge windows. The colour of the kitchen changes throughout the day and can be a deep green-blue in the bright morning light and a dark gunmetal blue in the evening. All the timbers were bought raw, then stained onsite to match the deep brown tones of winter. The rust and burnt orange tones are taken from the dusty dry landscape during summer.

How has your style evolved over the years?

For as long as I can remember I have loved earth tones and contrasting colour palettes. I have always instinctively played with colour combinations and how they make us feel. My style in both design and decoration is heavily driven by nature and a desire to merge living spaces with the colours and textures of the landscape that surrounds each home.

Texture is another big design element at Resident Avenue. Layering and exploring the different textures and patina of natural materials, and the way that they are constantly changing, plays an important role in all our interiors. Each project has a strong thread of handmade elements, and we work alongside many skilled craftspeople and artisans, collaborating to design bespoke details for each home.

I am also passionate about mixing old with new. Carefully curated antiques or worldly treasures are combined with textural rugs and modern interiors to tell a story. Travel and exposure to other cultures provide new lenses to reflect on the way we live, and the diverse way others live: the memories, colours, landscape and smells overload the senses, sparking new design ideas.

Do you have a favourite colour, pattern or similar that you often turn to?

Chartreuse olive green is my all-time fav; yes, of course, it has a mustard undertone! Our antique office table here at RA is painted in 2pac acrylic paint in this colour. But it is nature that remains the primary thread of inspiration for me, so patterns or colours that are reflective of nature are often incorporated into our designs. Materials in their raw form – full of character, elemental and evolving – are something that we always turn to. Corten steel features in many of our projects for this reason. Its strong colour and ever-changing form is art in itself. Timeless and naturally aged substrates create contrasting tones to blend with textural fabrics and tribal patterns. Layering these patterns and textures brings warmth and depth into the home and delivers a uniquely curated result.

How do you incorporate colour into your home?

I love blending texture and colour in compelling and sometimes unexpected ways. I start with a hard surface material base in a refined earthy palette and then create layers and colour combinations with vibrant soft furnishings, artwork, rugs, textiles and sculptures. The combinations and layering are made to look effortless when, in fact, it has been quite the opposite.

I am a big believer in helping people understand that colour is timeless. I think that's why I love 'dirty' colours – to me, they are like neutrals, a timeless base that works with almost any other colour you can imagine. These base colours give room for additions and change as your life evolves.

Thoughtful design is about encouraging this, daring people to try new things, to trust their instinct and create a home that is unique to them.

Do you have a favourite item at home?

I have a large collection of small treasures that I have gathered over the years and that are part of my family's journey. If I really had to 'grab and go' there is a large, handblown dusty pink glass vessel from Biot in the South of France that I would run through flames to save. My mother and father spent much of their twenties and thirties with friends in that region. This vessel evokes treasured memories that link to family and friends. I carried this particular piece in my hand luggage on a three-week trip around Europe! It is these items, the ones that are part of my story, that I love the most.

How does colour influence the way you live?

I couldn't cope without it in my life. It's everywhere I turn and essential to my being. From my wardrobe, to the art hanging in my house, to the crockery I use every day – I surround myself with the colours and textures I love.

Colour plays a big part in my mood and it dictates how I feel when I walk into a room or how I want to spend time in a space. It's a powerful tool in design and communication. I want my home to be a warm, relaxed and engaging space and let the colours tell our family story.

Who or what inspires you?

Coming from a background in fashion, it would be hard to say that I'm not inspired by textiles. My early career was spent working for high-end fashion label Trelise Cooper. Trelise is a strong, passionate and creative woman, and her label is known for vibrant colours and clashing of beautiful prints. It was definitely a formative influence and contributed to me developing my ability to see unusual colour combinations and mix prints and patterns.

My mother is and will always be my biggest inspiration. She is a dynamic, clever, creative and passionate woman. She is the reason I believe in myself and the reason I am confident to trust my intuition.

In the design world I am in awe of Patricia Urquiola. If I come across a tile or a piece of furniture that I fall in love with, it is almost always a Patricia Urquiola design! Her designs are textural, unexpected and although strong in form, they often have a playful accent that just makes me smile.

Do you have a favourite location or place to visit and why?

Byron Bay. My best friend, and a collection of other treasured friends and family all live there. Byron is definitely my home away from home and the place where I find my mind is truly still (which it isn't very often). The beach, the fresh air, the personal connections and laughter are how I recharge and reset.

COLOUR CRAZE

Crisp all-white rooms – white walls, white billowy curtains and crisp ivory bed linen – do feel quiet and peaceful, really rather dreamlike. I can appreciate their pure form for a while, but then I also often have a sense that something is not quite right. The 'a-ha' moment is, of course, that the space is missing colour.

The beauty of colour is certainly always in the eye of the beholder. Its subjective nature means that what one person likes, another won't. Once you have nutted out what colours are right for you, it's a matter of where and how to add them into the mix. Here are some tips to get you started.

1 – FIND YOUR COLOURS

Colour, and how much you use it, is entirely personal. There is no right or wrong, but the key is to commit to it.

Try using variations of your colour choices as accents throughout a home to create a considered and unified look; for example, if blue is a key colour in your interior, you can continue the palette with teals and greens. Further visual appeal can also be achieved by incorporating textured fabrics and finishes – linen, timber or stone can all diversify a consistent aesthetic.

Of course, contrasting colours can create even more visual interest. If you are not confident to mix colour combinations, colour authority Pantone has created an app, My Pantone, which does it for you. It takes the science out of colour selections and offers advice on complementary colour schemes.

2 – UNDERSTAND INDUSTRY TERMS

Terms such as tint, tone and shade are regularly referred to when discussing all things colour. It's worthwhile getting to know what these terms mean. That way, you'll have a better understanding of applying colour in all its forms to your interiors.

Essentially, tints, tones and shades refer to the variations in colour when white, black or grey are mixed in.

A tint is a lighter version of a colour, created by adding white, and can be quite calming. Pastels are a good example of this.

A shade is a darker version of a colour, created by adding black. Navy – the result of adding black to blue – is a classic shade.

Tones denote the addition of both black and white (grey) to a colour and can be darker or lighter than the original hue depending on the proportions of grey added. Often referred to as muted tones, these hues are more subtle than tints and shades.

3 – TAKE YOUR TIME

If you are a little afraid of colour, go slow, go small. Add measured amounts of it to start with and live with it for a while before deciding on how much more to add or subtract.

As you grow in confidence and you learn what works for you and what doesn't, you'll be waving your colour wand with authority.

4 – HAVE A PLAN
Before you start, think about the mood you want to create in each space. For instance, if you are after peace and tranquillity in the bedroom, avoid bright colours. Colour can turn the volume up or down, so use it to your advantage.

5 – ALLOW COLOUR TO POP
Think about going for dark walls rather than white. While a white wall will certainly provide contrast for bold colours that are used throughout your furnishings and decor, and have a fresh feel, a moody hue will showcase colour even better.

6 – VARIATIONS OF HUE
If colour mixing isn't your thing, it can be equally as effective to stick with a single hue. If you prefer just one colour, try using it in different shades for maximum impact. For instance, a graduated ombre effect can be very striking and is always complementary.

7 – TIMELESS COMBINATIONS
If you feel bright colours are a bit too much for you, opt for more timeless combinations such as black and white, which still pack a punch decoratively and tend not to date.

8 – TRY SOMETHING NEW
While tried-and-true colour combinations do work supremely well, at times something more imaginative is called for. In fact, more unexpected combinations can work incredibly well, and often a soft mixed with a bold packs some extra punch; think terracotta teamed with cobalt, or teal mixed with mustard. One of my go-to combinations is a soft duck-egg blue and a punchy chartreuse – this is a surprising combination that seriously rocks my world. It's all about these hues being total opposites – and opposites attracting. I need only think of one of my favourite decor pieces, a two-toned velvet cushion, to be reminded of how well this unlikely duo works together.

9 – TRIPLE TREAT
Art is a wonderful focal point with which to ground a space. You can make any room feel well thought out by pulling out colours from an artwork; that, in turn, will make your colour choices feel more cohesive. Then repeat that colour in three places for unison in the room.

Watch the sky or sea, the shifting patterns and shades of blues, and it is easy to understand why blue is so well loved. Earth is a blue planet, and the colour exerts an almost physical pull on the human eye. It is considered peaceful and calming, and is undoubtedly a colour that people find tranquil, restorative and easy to live with.

'A certain blue enters your soul,' said painter Henri Matisse, a confident colourist after my own heart, and just one artist who has shown an enduring love for this colour range. Historically, the use of blue in architecture, heraldry, art and decoration has been associated with loyalty, wisdom, faith and truth. Today, it is most commonly associated with harmony.

The blue palette available in decor is enormous. The difficulty is deciding whether you're drawn to deep blues such as navy, the evocatives (indigo, peacock, cornflower) or the paler pastel tones. Or build layers of different shades of blue, grounding it with neutrals, lifting it with a snap of contrast.

As a cool colour, blue is compatible with other cooler hues, such as grey. For higher contrasts, try it with warmer accents – red, coral or yellow. It is a strong foundation colour and versatile throughout the home, without shouting.

For a serene feel, cerulean shades are an ideal choice for a bedroom setting. Try a calming sky-blue wall paired with lighter to neutral shades in other details, such as crisp white bedding. If you're looking for something less permanent, consider a sophisticated midnight-blue headboard as the feature piece, or simple turquoise soft furnishings for a gem-like pop.

Blue is much loved as a feature colour in living room settings. A sofa in any shade of blue – think navy or a rich sapphire – can be a beautiful grounding piece around which your decor is based. Of course, blue is just about a must-have in coastal themed interiors where, alongside clean whites and natural textures, it is a classic combination.

Don't overlook the use of blue in the kitchen, whether yours is contemporary, provincial or has a country vibe. Incorporate blue tones or use it as a key feature – think a teal tiled splashback, or even pastel cabinetry. Blue can add personality without being overbearing. On a smaller scale, consider ceramics or tableware for subtle bursts of colour.

Make it regal by pairing it with gold or make it breezy by combining it with white and natural tones, and be assured it lends itself to both small- and large-scale applications.

← Different shades and tones of blue provide rhythm and repetition in this kitchen and living area. Gleaming blue wall tiles, in an irregular layout, are a sublime backdrop for the white cabinetry. The neutral chequered flooring brings warmth – like bleached fields.

↑ It makes sense to draw on the colours of the natural world when looking for design inspiration. Referencing key colours of your surrounds creates a harmonious connection between indoors and out – in this case the vivid blue of the sky and water.

A punchy cobalt coffee table, like a hunk of semi-precious lapis lazuli stone, creates visual interest and is an assured choice as a focal point. Create colour cohesion through other tones and patterns of blue – or leave one knockout piece as a standalone colour statement.

A blue palette is a trusty all-rounder, with enduring appeal in coastal, country and provincial-style interiors. Washed-out blues and greens together are a winning combination regardless of style or period.

The blue tiled floor immediately cools this summer space down.

→ While it is perhaps more commonly associated with neutrals, blue also is a friend to warmer accents such as red, coral or yellow. Here, every item demands attention thanks to the high contrast – there's no homogenous colour palette.

← Blue is a strong foundation colour that is incredibly versatile. It is an ideal backdrop to influences from different eras, from traditional to contemporary.

↑ Traditional pairings, like cobalt blue and terracotta, or the blues and whites synonymous with Morocco or Greece, continue to provide inspiration to travellers and artists. The combinations still have a place in today's interiors as we pay tribute to these ancient associations in our decor.

← Why restrict pattern and colour to living areas? A palette of blue, brown and cream, with dark timber and a quirky collection of shells and sponges, is echoed in a classic Chinoiserie wallpaper, adding interest to a small space.

←← A mere hint of colour is sometimes all that is required to enhance a space, as achieved here with small splashes of china blue to brighten the outdoor shower area.

↑ Never underestimate the power of a patterned ceiling – paint, wallpaper or timber. Some of the most interesting homes play on this role reversal by flipping flooring to ceiling. This technique also draws the eye up, which can give the illusion of a higher room.

→ Inky dark blue adds mood. If you want to be cocooned, take the same colour from the floor to the walls and then all the way to the ceiling.

Mariella Ienna

Palermo, Italy

Tell us a little about creating this space. What was it inspired by?

It is located in the historic centre of Palermo, Sicily, in a fourteenth-century convent building, part of the San Domenico Church and monastery complex. It was an abandoned roof space with 14-foot rafted ceilings, infested with pigeons (and that many years of dung). Being a heritage-classified building, the space was inspired by the need for the new steel 'tower' structure to be respectful of the tufa walls and not close off the open space and height. And I just wanted to continue to marvel up close at walls that had been laid five hundred years ago. The fact that cloistered nuns lived here (and apparently made marzipan sweets in their spare moments) also imbues the space with a lovely energy.

Have you always loved colour?

I have always used colour sparingly, and with an instinctive rather than deliberate style.

My inclination is to start with natural elements, textures and colours, and use colour to highlight rather than dominate the elements.

I used to work with flowers and organic materials (my studio in Sydney was called Verdant Flower Merchants) and actually preferred to work with leaves, branches and dried organic materials rather than flowers per se.

My favourite colours would have to be indigo, and a Sicilian type of 'antico' green, and dull gold that is used in many of the noble villas. And agave grey-blue.

Do you have a favourite item at home?

My favourite items are mainly found objects that I have transformed with colour (well, usually black) or my textural fabrics, such as the long black bench upholstered with kilim fabric that is in my kitchen. I found this piece sticking up out of a council bin and called my upholsterer to retrieve it.

How has your style evolved over the years?

I have been influenced by Sicilian Norman and Baroque decorative and architectural traditions, which surround me in Palermo. Syracuse and Modica are also favourite places of inspiration. I have found that, when these designs are metabolised and simplified they become surprisingly contemporary. Mediterranean plants also inspire me hugely; now, and even before I lived in Sicily, it was as if a kind of genetic memory and predilection existed within me for Bismarckia palms, agave fronds, papyrus and bleached tufa stone. Creatively everything made sense for me once I moved here.

Who or what inspires you?

All artisans inspire me and teach me; in this home, my carpenters, ebonists, steel workers and upholsterers and I can say that every element has been artisan-made in a collaborative approach to restoration, and mutual exchange of skills and aesthetics.

India is also important for me creatively. Indian artisans rule supreme in my eyes. My carpets and textiles are realised in the Panipat (Delhi) and Badohoi/Varanasi regions. I visit India almost monthly and its creative pulse sustains me too. My work here is very much a collaboration. It is artisan but it is also accessible and mass produced. Only in India have they managed to produce hundreds of metres of carpets by hand and yet with consistency.

I am thrilled each time to start with an idea, and the producers and their weavers, more often than not, take that somewhere else with their materials and their creative instincts as to what might be best for the design. I love this element of surprise, randomness, alchemy, synergy, destiny, whatever you like to call it.

A LOOK FOR ALL SEASONS

Every season offers its own delights: the simple joys of curling up in front of an autumn fire, rugging up for a wintery walk, or witnessing an explosion of spring colour before the transition to summer. It's all about embracing the seasonal changes – in weather and customs – and taking cues from Mother Nature.

When it comes to the seasons, I unashamedly admit to loving the warmth, vibrancy and bright tones of summer. But as the cooler months approach, I do say goodbye to balmy summer evenings and welcome the magic of the change of season.

These changes can be embraced within your own four walls too. Consider these hints to styling for your home to reflect the best of every season.

WINTER WONDERS

Create a feeling of winter cosiness by ensuring your house is full of comforts that cocoon you in warmth, whether through colour, texture or even scent.

Introducing darker colours is an effective way to work in with a wintery feel. Even the simplest changes can have an impact – you don't have to paint the walls or buy new furniture to achieve a cool-season palette, but concentrate on smaller, more affordable items.

In winter it is textiles such as cushions, throws and bed linen that set the scene. Layering in textures like chunky wool knits, faux fur and cord will give a rich depth to interiors.

We know the warming glow from an open fire casts its own beautiful light, but a similar ambience can be created by using dimmers on lights, or candles.

Winter is a time to appeal to *all* the senses, so don't overlook the smell; a pot simmering on the stove harnesses all the best savoury cool-season aromas, or you could invest in a room spray that evokes the smell of burning wood if you don't own a fireplace (I recommend Diptyque's Feu de Bois room spray).

SPRING FLING

Spring is all about rejuvenation. And while the outdoors is abuzz with new life, this same feel can also be achieved indoors.

Introduce a fresh ambience inside the home by packing away the heavy fabrics until next year, throwing open the windows and doors, and making the most of the season by adding as many vessels of sweetly scented blooms as you can. It can be as simple as one daffodil in the bathroom.

Moody hues should be replaced with a lighter colour palette, and crisp whites interspersed with bursts of brighter hues work beautifully.

Spring is the season for new beginnings, an ideal time to complete that paint job you've been contemplating, or even reconfiguring your artwork or furniture for a fresh look.

This season is about emerging from your winter hibernation, enjoying the changing light and opening up that indoor-outdoor connection.

SUMMER LOVING

Most quintessential Australian imagery depicts sunshine, beaches and outdoor activities and, for many, the relaxed vibes of summer are what it's all about.

You can express that chilled feeling in the styling of summer interiors too. As the warmer days approach, consider paring back your interiors to ensure that breezy indoor-outdoor connection is optimised.

Bring the outdoors in with tropical-inspired botanicals like leafy palms and ferns – either featuring specimens in pots indoors, or their motif in fabrics and tableware. Try

to get as much natural light into your indoor spaces as possible, without too much harsh direct light to burn your plants or fade your fabrics.

When it comes to a summer palette, opt for lighter colours. For textures, think sisal rugs and 'flowy' sheer curtains. Linen, too, is a summer staple thanks to its soft, organic texture and feel.

If you are a true colour lover, now is your moment to go bold with the accents in your home. Fiery orange, sunny yellow, pink flamingo and coral are all fabulous options. Be sure to commit to your colour choice: you want it to feel considered rather than accidental. Try threading accents of one colour in varying degrees throughout your home for a unified feel.

Generous bowls of edible fruits are a simple option for delivering that burst of happy seasonal colour.

While air and light are key summer themes, water is also a central element thanks to its cooling powers and the refreshing vibe it brings. If you don't have a pool, invest in a freestanding outdoor shower and throw a summery towel over the fence or nearby tree.

Water features and water gardens are ways to introduce acoustic watery pleasure and a stunning focal point on a deck or patio.

AUTUMNAL TONES

As nature puts on its spectacular colour-changing show, the cooler temperatures are also a trigger for interiors to move from light and airy to warm and cosy.

For autumnal interiors I am immediately drawn to the earthy, warm tones that are reflected in the outdoors. Rusty oranges, rich plums, clarets, umber and terracotta hues work beautifully indoors and trigger something akin to nesting in me.

But it's not just the colours of the season that can influence your interiors. My favourite thing to do when autumn hits is to bring those magical, crunchy leaves inside and create displays with them, or use seed heads and twisted fallen branches for structure, in ochre, chocolate and greys.

Complement these beautiful seasonal botanicals with flora and fauna prints, while hits of natural fibres found in woven baskets, woollen rugs and other textural accessories add tactile character.

Balance the earthiness with a touch of the refined. Gold, brass or copper metallics all work well with an autumn palette and add glamour and warmth to a space.

When it comes to styling for the season, it's not about reconfiguring your entire home. Let Mother Nature dictate your theme, and work with what is already on offer. The smallest of touches are enough to hint that the season has changed.

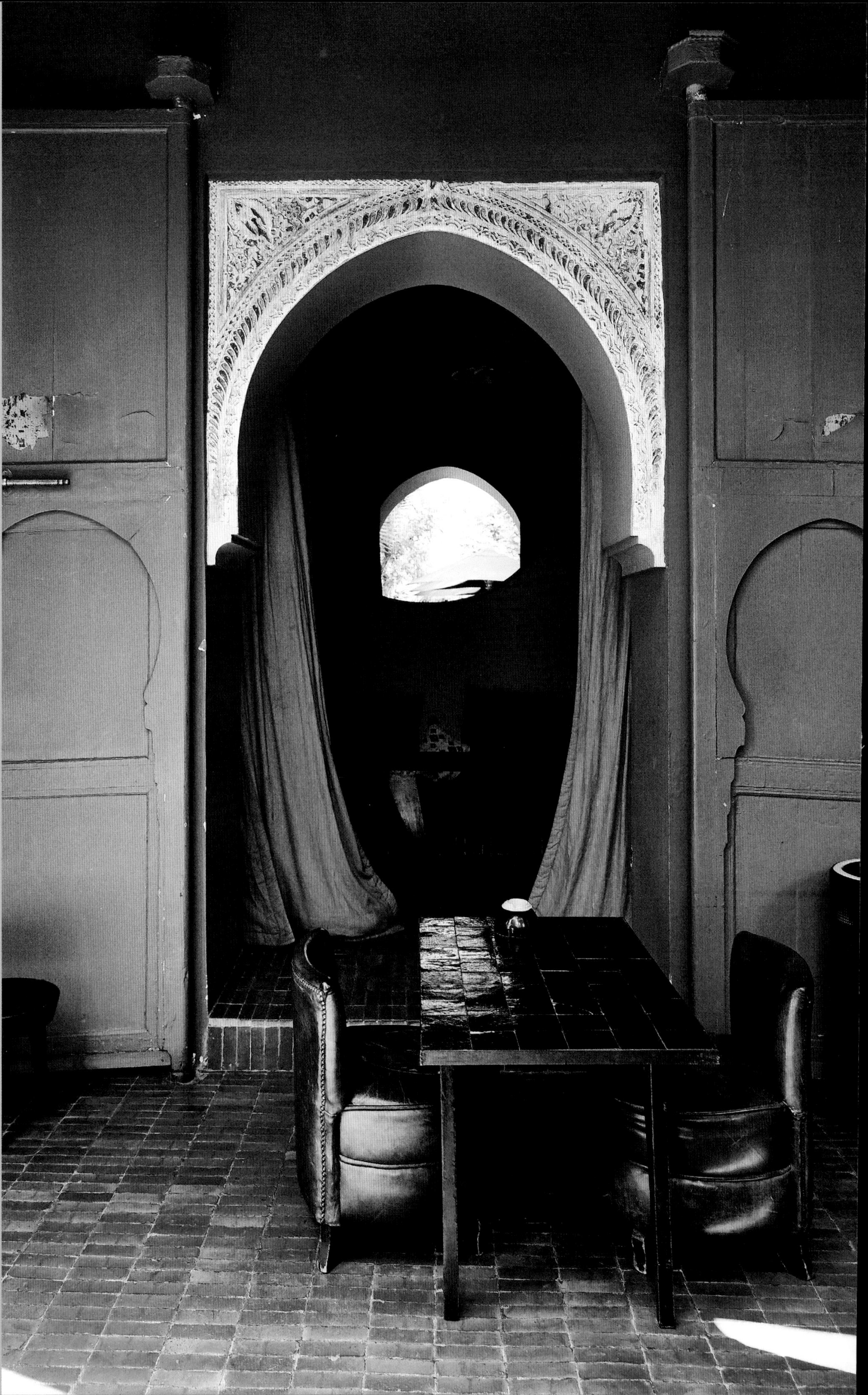

For me, beautiful interiors are those where space has been given to colour from the outset. Colour signals the spirit of the place just as much as the possessions and backstories embedded in our homes.

My own favourite colour is green – lush, flecked valleys and tendrils of it feature in my house. It symbolises the essence of life, and I get a real charge from its positive energy in my home.

Many of nature's life-affirming cues are green. Think new spring growth, the deep greens of forest canopies, manicured lawns or the viridian of the ocean, dark and turbulent on a stormy day. Our eye might also be caught by a greenhouse bursting with ferns, a perfect zesty lime or a tumble of greens in the garden.

While we are clearly drawn to greens in nature, our connection with the colour can find expression in our homes as well. Consider reproducing that intense green-blue of late evening light in your home, or the shade of cool mint, or maybe a dignified olive tone.

Go bold with a rich emerald green sofa in a living space, or gleaming pickle-green tiling – mosaic, glass, ornate – in a bathroom or kitchen. Sage or olive carpet can look fabulous, and the right shade is calming and restful in bedrooms, particularly if paired with neutral linens. For something less permanent, you could try a green rug or runner, emerging in a space like an oasis.

Allow forest tones to work with timber or metallics for a harmonious combination of natural elements – the weathered look of patina is especially attractive.

Apply green in solid blocks or shades. For a subtle touch, decorative pieces such as moss-toned glassware and ceramics can provide just the right amount of interest. Artworks, too, can unify elements of an interior. Look out for landscapes and botanical or floral paintings and prints with complementary tones.

And, of course, indoor plants can provide a glorious injection of colour. There is nothing like an array of healthy plants – themselves a shot of colour, but with equal wow from the pots – to add interest and a living, breathing component to your room.

Most of the colour wheel considers versatile green a friend because it can be layered brilliantly as an accent or as a full-blown feature. In my opinion, every interior is better for at least a hint of it.

← There is no need to be a colour purist with green – just as in nature, mixing up shades works. Different tones and tints together evoke a leafy garden, forest or shady oasis and can be adopted in your own home. To ground this mix, though, use solid dark- or light-coloured furniture.

← The impact of light – natural and supplementary – will always affect your choice of colour, so within less well-lit spaces, be prepared for green to take on even deeper hues. In brighter spaces, the exact same colour will perform differently. Be sure to think about lighting when you're selecting a colour scheme.

↑ Consider a touch of cooling green in your flooring – ceramic tiling, painted or stencilled floorboards, or a modern patterned vinyl. Mint works for a retro look, but you may prefer a mossy tone or an almost turquoise shade underfoot. Unlike walls that can be easily repainted, flooring is quite an investment, so consider your choice carefully.

Aged surfaces have a romantic appeal, especially as the bones of a space. This green-and-white flooring is busy, but works because it is balanced by block-coloured walls and the solid whites in the flowing linen. The deliberate contrast is unifying.

→ Look to unexpected places for opportunities to accentuate colour. This room features a large block wall of burnt orange against a softer green floor, but there is also clever repetition in the two orange painted doorway insets, subtle staging for what lies within.

Apple green is punchy and fabulous as an accent every time. It steps right up against neutral tones such as ash flooring, or the blush of stucco-like walls, and nearby plantings add a bit more green texture and body.

Green cabinetry and joinery is a confident use of colour and works best within a neutral frame of white, black or grey.

When considering tiling half or painting half of a wall, ensure the
room has reasonably high ceilings to avoid it feeling cut in half.
Or don't work strictly with halves: try thirds. Painting the ceiling
ensures the space feels whole.

Never underestimate the power of a coloured front door, or the effect
of coloured trims on a home. The Europeans have been doing it for
centuries, and such colour instantly welcomes you and your guests
home, to a happy place.

A mirror has always been a clever way to enlarge a space by multiplying its reflection. Mirrors can also be used to lighten an interior, extend a vista and create a focal point, whether wall-mounted or ceiling-scale.

This small but striking green window vignette draws you right in among an otherwise deliberately neutral room. Small uses of colour can be just as impactful as saturated colour.

Willem Smit

El Fenn, Marrakech, Morocco

Tell us a little about creating this space. What was it inspired by?
The bones of the hotel's design were created by the original owners, Howell James and Vanessa Branson. They used only local artisans and traditional techniques such as zellige tiling and hand-mixed tadelakt lime plaster in strong, bold colours when they refurbished a derelict riad that housed El Fenn's first six rooms. Into this, they added a mix of mid-century European furniture and art from Vanessa's private collection.

When I arrived to manage El Fenn in 2011, I developed the look over the next few years as I refurbished every part of the hotel before adding new rooms, knocking down walls and really maximising what we had here. I can never sit still, and we also have a lot of regular guests so I want people who know the hotel to always find something new when they return.

Have you always loved colour?
No! In my own homes, I stick to a pretty stripped-back palette. But El Fenn had an established look, and colour was a key part of that. I've pulled it back to a core of hot pink, teal, ochre and red, but it wasn't hard for me to embrace colour because that's what people who stay at El Fenn expect. Colour also works well in Morocco because of the amazing light.

How has your style evolved over the years?
My style has evolved because I've learned more about art and design, and these two things are now really important to me. I've learned a lot more about African art, for instance, since living in Morocco and have invested in some beautiful work for my own home. But there are also some key parts of my style that have always been: I've always liked oversized pieces, groups of objects and sticking to a very limited core of one or two colours throughout a home.

Do you have a favourite colour, pattern or similar that you often turn to?
I always return to blue (particularly teals), a mustardy-gold ochre and olive green.

How do you incorporate colour into your home?
After all the colour and drama of El Fenn, my own home is painted white. I need that simplicity after a day at work. I add in colour using fabrics, but it's very limited because I don't want anything to shout at me.

Do you have a favourite item at home?
An antique walnut desk that I bought in Barcelona; my Eames chair; a limited-edition Helmut Newton Sumo book; my grandfather's army trunk; a collection of black-and-white pictures of family and friends; and my art, which I look at every day.

How does colour influence the way you live?
I think of colour as a beautiful base to highlight art, objects, antiques and design.

Who or what inspires you?
Interior designers Ilse Crawford and Lázaro Rosa-Violán; Samuel Deshors, the production designer of the film *Call Me By Your Name*; and French architects Studio KO.

TRENDS AND CLASSICS

Whether you are a colour lover or pick from a minimal palette, whether your preference is for Scandi or coastal style, or even if it's a mishmash of themes, interiors have never been more personalised than they are right now.

And yet, trends are a reality that affect all parts of our cultural life. There are no hard and fast rules when it comes to styling your space, but what is true is that every era – actually, every design and fashion season – brings its own influences. Some endure longer than others, but who knows what will prove to be a classic and what is nothing more than a flash in the pan? Oh, to have a crystal ball. In the end, regardless of the trend of a moment or even decade, only you can be the one to decide if a colour stays or goes.

Even though I have my favourite go-to colours and combinations, I am always interested in new trends. I get a kick out of thinking about their application and their companion or contrast colours. I like to ponder what colours we can expect to dominate interiors, but that interest does not always have to translate to application. It's ok for trends to simply be admired from afar.

What about classics? Although it can be hard to predict the future – but inevitable we will rework the past – there are some foolproof combinations that stand the test of time. Classical black-and-white stripes have never dated and likely never will. French navy and cream feels timeless as well as elegant, as does a trusted duck-egg blue, which lends itself to be paired with other fresh pastels or bold brights that happen to come or go over time. All of these combinations are considered good neutrals too. They are bound to go with whatever the new trend happens to be, and are what you would call a safe choice.

With the inevitable overlap between fashion and interiors, it makes sense to look to the catwalks for colour forecasts and predictors of colour trends. Given the emergence of COVID-19, though, and the unprecedented amount of armchair travel as opposed to real-time travel, it will be interesting to see what impact this has globally for future colour predictions.

The popularity of stylised florals and bold African patterns in fashion means that these same combinations and clashes of bright colours will likely find their way into homes before long.

These trends are also apparent in the art scene. Large oversized floral compositions and serene captures of botanicals will power on, adding signs of life to interior spaces and walls by linking the outdoors to inside.

In terms of colours, it is a sea-inspired palette that I expect to have a strong influence in the near future. As people strive to disconnect from the distractions of their busy lives and become lost in their own peaceful surrounds, all shades of calming blue and green will have a place in contemporary interiors.

Like anything style related, interior trends are, of course, subjective. While some may embrace eclectic patterns and palettes with enthusiasm, others may introduce them gently.

Don't be afraid to add a little bit of daring and individuality to the interior mix – it doesn't have to be permanent. Trends will come and go, and if you don't love it, you won't want to live with it. Draw on what speaks to you.

Pink

Colour is not just to be seen, but to be felt. I learnt this credo from my mother, and I am still guided by it. It's up to each of us to work out our colours.

Pink evokes an emotional response in me. I experience all sorts of sentimental triggers when surrounded by the calming serenity of blush or the flamboyance of flamingo. Pink has been a stand-in for all things feminine for over fifty years but, pleasingly, it has been liberated from the 'girls department' and is more widely used across the board.

Hot pink is synonymous with playfulness, and bubble-gum and magenta shades suggest a party atmosphere. Yet there are so many variations in pink, all the way to soothing rose and pastel tones; indeed, the colour range is known for its calming, therapeutic effects and feel-good message.

Pinks are fresh and versatile in interiors, with intense shades such as fuchsia or raspberry adding a flash of glamour alongside deep green or even black. Paler shades – if I say ballet pinks you'll know what I mean – look fabulous when used with a bold primary contrast such as yellow, red or apple green.

Dusty or chalky salmon pink is elegant and reminiscent of an art deco golden age; this end of the pink range is gentle and sophisticated, far from babyish or brassy. It is easily picked up in accompanying artwork – think large, abstract/tonal works – or as a lampshade atop a bronze or clear base. Other combinations I love are musk with a golden brown and charcoal with dirty pink.

Once a go-to for soft furnishings only, pink is now widely used in everything from wall colours to lighting, statement furniture pieces and even large appliances – a pastel pink fridge, anyone?

Pink's versatility means creating a look you love is easier than you might think. A pink sofa, for example, works wonderfully with the warmth of timber, whether in flooring or furniture, but equally it can provide a lovely contrast against hard, industrial finishes such as concrete. Metallics, too, are a beautiful complement – pink seating paired with a copper coffee table can make a stunning statement in a living space, as can blush bathroom accessories alongside brass or copper tapware.

Pink as a foil to hard surfaces is a revelation. One of the most successful interiors I have seen featured an oversized rug in a delicate pink taffy hue, alongside a sizeable red brick wall. The pink softened the space, perfectly juxtaposed to the solid surface. An inspired combination.

While pink is still regarded as a feminine colour, it is no longer exclusively so. I urge you to consider its many charms.

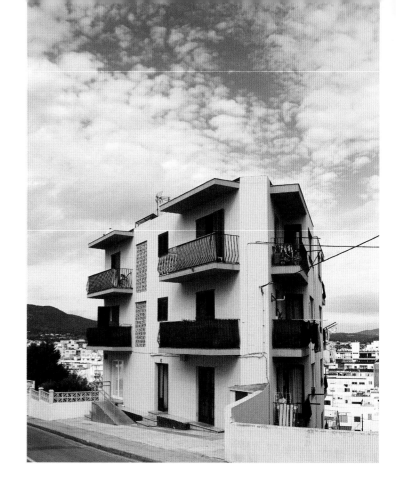

←← Red and pink: in my opinion, it's one of the most powerful combinations. This sweet combo is best used in neutral surrounds, to avoid lolly overload, and restraint is called for too; a cushion or, in this instance, artwork are statement enough.

← Clever lighting – such as the addition of recessed fluoro pink hall lights that cast shadows to the wall and ceiling – can add an artful and unconventional twist to an entryway, allowing you to enjoy a white or pink hallway.

→ Rooms that carry off pattern-on-pattern successfully show commitment to the cause, but it is important to have somewhere for the eye to rest. If you have maximalist tendencies, try to find one place in the room that breaks the pattern, allowing the space to breathe.

← Calming pink is an excellent choice for bedrooms – both in old and contemporary homes – but to avoid it feeling overly feminine, look to counterbalance the shade with some bolder contrasting pieces, such as a statement chair or a strong rug to ground it.

↑ Two-toned walls that share the same family of colour are a smart way to create impact without hanging art. This can be an economical way of creating colour interest without taking hammer and nail to your walls. It is the extension of colour to the ceiling that completes this room.

Laurence Leenaert

Marrakech, Morocco

Tell us a little about creating this space. What was it inspired by?
My home in Gueliz, Marrakech, is a very small house but it has high white walls and I add colour with paintings, photos and textiles.

I made almost all the furniture and chose the colours for the textiles we used for the furniture. I try to keep the look a bit neutral so there is not too much going on and to give a calm feeling. The studio is colourful; the house is softer and less busy.

Have you always loved colour?
Yes – and since I moved to Marrakech and now live under the sun, colours became even more important. The colours are more vivid here: I'm surrounded by palm trees, pink walls, people wearing oversized, coloured djellabas – people here are not scared of colour.

I also love taking photos and playing with the colours of the objects, subjects, light. Light is influencing.

How has your style evolved over the years?
I have always been inspired by graphic design and creating shapes in space in a kind of naïve way. My style is largely still the same, but evolving too I think – I try to challenge myself.

Do you have a favourite colour, pattern or similar that you often turn to?
Nude and earth tones and, of course, Morocco's famous Majorelle blue; it gives so much power.

How do you incorporate colour into your home?
Textiles are very important and very present in the house. I love to have a white canvas and then bring colours together. I collect ceramics. I love wood and natural materials and then I add ceramics and wallpieces.

Do you have a favourite item at home?
I love the old tiles. The house is more than two hundred years old and is one of the oldest in Marrakech – you don't see a lot of them anymore in Gueliz.

How does colour influence the way you live?
Every day I'm busy with colours: combining colours and trying to make magic with them. It's interesting how colour can be so different in a material.

Who or what inspires you?
Travelling, art, my friends (friends and their habits are so interesting), colours, nature. It's all about the details.

Do you have a favourite location or place to visit and why?
At the moment I have a need to be around nature, no noise, far away from the chaos.

FLORALS AND BOTANICALS

The enduringly popular design theme of florals offers tremendous scope for colour. Whether delicate and whimsical, vibrant, playful or elegant, there is a place for botanical beauties in every home.

While the way we use florals may have changed over time – chintz textiles have been around since the seventeenth century – these beautiful motifs and patterns have never really been out of favour, as showcased in recent revivals of Florence Broadhurst and Marimekko.

Australian floral designs draw on native flora and landscapes, bringing the outdoors inside in a stylish way.

Thinking more broadly, some of my most adored designs offer a fresh, alternative take on traditional florals. Seed heads from pomegranates and poppies used in floral arrangements or in a print, for example, offer contrast in shape and texture and are wonderful options for incorporating a new take on the traditional.

Whether it's your forever piece, or something more subtle such as a dried flower arrangement, here are some ideas on how best to decorate your space to a floral theme.

IMPACT PIECES

Few prints are as versatile as botanicals, so if you're keen to go bold, florals are your friend. Consider the dramatic effect of a feature floral wall. A guest bedroom wall in my home has maximum visual impact thanks to a repeated image of hydrangeas, created using a photograph transferred onto wallpaper. You could also consider commissioning an artist to paint a wall mural for an abstract version of this interior design classic.

Other big-ticket items that lend themselves to floral patterns include sofas, curtains and rugs. A modern, patterned sofa or rug can make an artful centrepiece in a living space, and florals can offer interest while being a softer alternative to bolder patterns in window furnishings.

FLORAL ARTWORK

Floral artworks can take centre stage in any interior and can inform the rest of the palette from a decorating perspective. Working equally well in a bedroom or living room setting, taking colour cues from the works will build up an interesting and cohesive space. In a bedroom, this could be layers of linen in eucalyptus or dusty blush tones. Or find an unexpected colour in the art and add decorative accessories to highlight this for visual interest – think bolder hues such as yellow or orange for a stronger statement.

BEAUTIFUL BLOOMS

If you are less inclined to use artwork as your room's decorative focus, try introducing floral arrangements to a dresser or a bedside table in your bedroom, or a sideboard or dining table in living areas. There is little to rival the impact of a glorious bunch of fresh blooms in terms of colour, form and scent, adding a soft layer of pretty to any space. If you require more longevity, dried flowers are a logical choice and have made a comeback in interiors. Their form can add dimension and nostalgia to a space without being fusty.

ACCENT PIECES

A more subtle hint of floral can be achieved with soft furnishings; perhaps a cushion with a botanical print or bright floral print bedding. Texture can add extra punch too, as techniques such as embroidery, weaving and tufting all lend themselves to contemporary floral motifs.

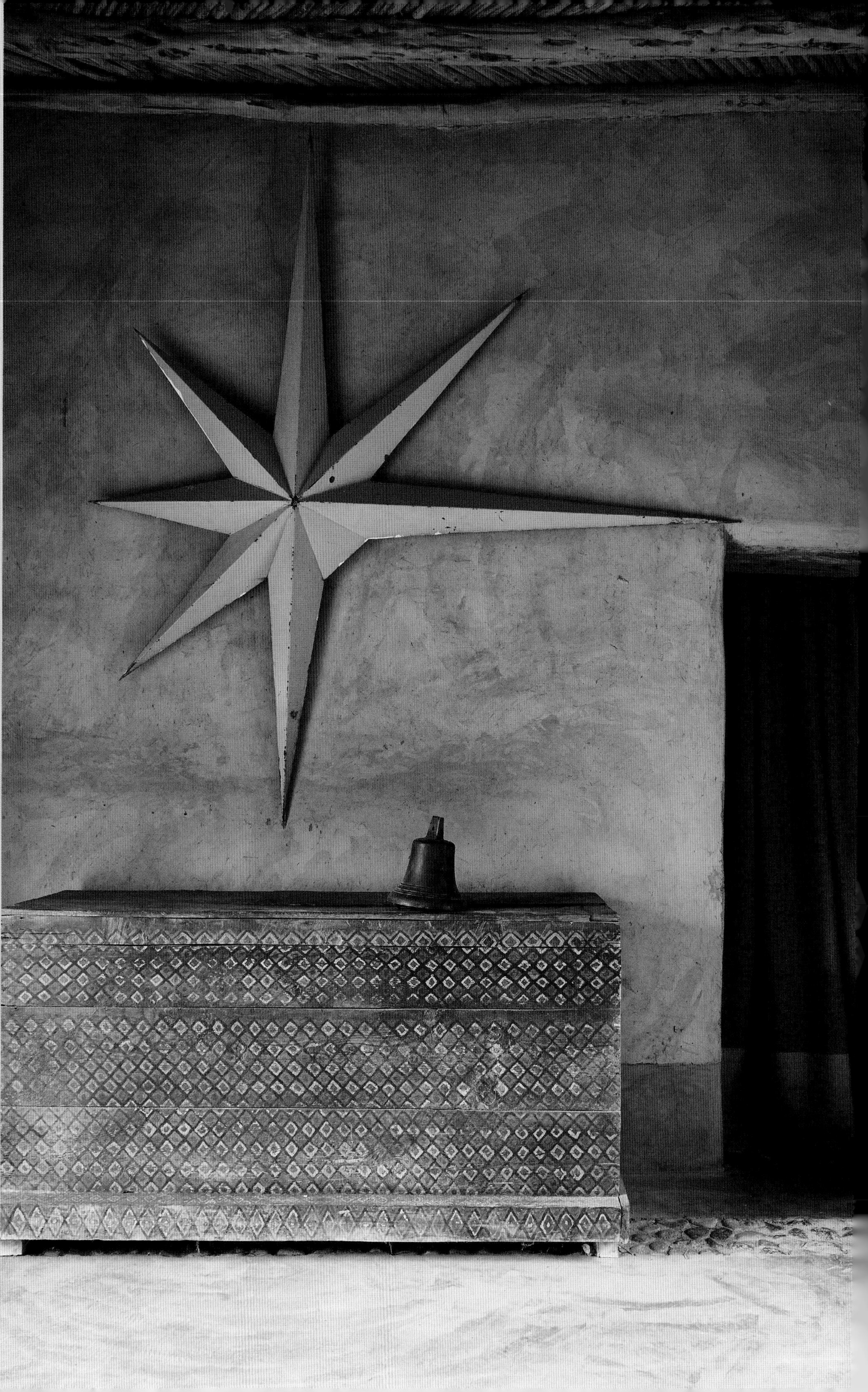

The cheerful qualities of yellow pack a positive punch in interiors, and those who know firsthand that its effects can be profound when it comes to happiness will use it in their repertoire with conviction. Don't for a moment think yellow is all high-vis or will dominate a space; those fears are unwarranted. The yellow palette ranges widely from bright and bold to sand, punchy sunflower and charming paler tones.

Synonymous with the colour of sunshine, yellow has always made me happy. To my mind, no other colour has the same uplifting ability.

Buttery shades are wonderful when used as accents in interiors, and bright pops of lemon in furnishings and decor items will add immediate visual interest to a space. A canary-coloured clock can turn a shelving display from drab to fab – but don't forget to include a mixture of heights for spatial contrast too. Complement yellow highlights in hung artworks or add cushions with contrasting texture and pattern.

Consider using darker yellows on a broader scale, with a luxe saffron or butterscotch sofa, sumptuous in velvet, or daffodil yellow dining chairs. A mustard-coloured feature wall might be just the tonic to stimulate both your space and your mind. I've seen it used to great effect in a study, offset by deep navy and neutral tones.

By the same token, warmer shades of honey and amber can add depth to a space when juxtaposed against cooler tones, thanks to their earthy natures. These darker shades – tending towards corn, ochre, gold – also look beautiful when used in an ombre effect, as the gradation of colour softens their impact.

Somewhat surprisingly, as a contrasting colour, yellow sits beautifully with white, orange, green, mauve and pink, all shades of blue, grey – right through to black.

In fact, it is one of the most glorious yet underused colours on the spectrum. I would love to see more of it applied in people's homes, if only for the cheeriness it fosters.

Yellow

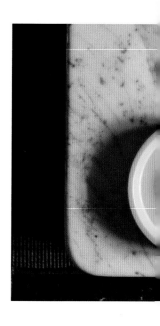

↑ Yellow surprises and delights in this playful powder room. Customised deep-lemon yellow tapware complements the heart motif wallpaper. Investigate customising your tapware if you long for more than the standard offerings, but of course, know that you need to commit to the colour for the long term.

→ Window furnishings can be one of the most powerful allies in the book of colour tricks. We're far too timid. Most of us play it pretty safe with neutrals because of the area to be covered. Here, however, luminous yellow shutters are like a ladder to the sun – and what a stunning afterglow.

Look-at-me yellow can be less confronting if used within a pattern such as a wallpaper or paired with natural materials such as raffia, beading or, indeed, wooden panelling or trims. It is like yellow's ego comes down a notch when it is faced with other elements of the natural world.

I've observed that those who use yellow in their decor are usually maximalists by inclination. For minimalists or those somewhere in the middle, start small. Consider a wall or a section of one before introducing more.

← Hardcore yellow fans prepared to match bold for bold will love a purple pairing. Yellow and purple are complementary colours, decadent and regal together. Keep it warm and use a golden yellow.

↑ Should your space allow it, consider using separate wall treatments for different zones. Here, a glowing golden wallpaper abuts a smoky blue wall, a gentle pairing that brings to mind dusk and dawn.

Vivid egg-yolk yellow is – granted – not for everyone, but when it joins forces with softer members of the rainbow, such as pale pink, powder blue or sage green, it can be right at home. Fun and carefree, the glossy yellow orb fits beautifully in this modernist interior.

Chartreuse, a delicious lime-green yellow, is at the top of my must-use list within interiors. It is alive, energised, and one of the best colour companions you could ask for – I think it works with any colour on the wheel. I urge you to try this crisp, almost tangy colour, which pastel and bright love equally, even if it starts with some glassware or a book spine or two. You will be rewarded handsomely.

Colour layering, when used successfully, draws your eye to all the right places: a feature bedhead, a mustardy velvet couch, a smooth yellow chair. They're unified by the fall of light from both sides of the room – for me, the overall effect is optimistic and dramatic. The heightened impact of the yellow against the darkened surrounds is well worth noting here.

→ Don't be held back by the fear of using yellow. Remember to test the waters with one object in a space and if it calls your name, add to it in a careful and considered manner. If your response to a colour is to paint the entire room, listen to that gut feeling. Colour is just that: a feeling.

Eryca Green
and Edward Opmanis

Melbourne, Australia

Tell us a little about creating this space. What was it inspired by?

This is an ever-evolving space. The house has been in Eddy's family for sixty years and he grew up here. The fig tree and apple tree in the garden were planted by his parents, although the rest of the garden has been done by me. There have been two renovations over the past fifteen years and further work is required. Add to that the sentimentality of a family home, two people coming together later in life with their own styles and stuff, the necessity of sticking within a tightish budget, and all you can do is throw your hands up in the air and experiment like crazy until decisions can be made like whether to knock it down or to renovate. It means we are a bit in limbo, but with that comes this incredible freedom to use the whole place like a mood board.

Have you always loved colour?

Yes, even when it was profoundly unfashionable to do so. Even my photographic work is predominantly colourful. White walls terrify me! Eddy has had to be brought around to colour though. It has been brave of him – albeit often very reluctantly – to allow me to bring so much colour into the home.

How has your style evolved over the years?

Once you get to our age, you would hope that your style has evolved several times! The fact that we don't have children living at home allows for a different approach now. As we amass knowledge on the furniture we work with, our style evolves with the learning. Knowledge is a wonderful thing. It gives perspective and understanding, which can change how you view something. My tastes have changed and refined. There are pieces I would have thought ugly ten years ago, but I can now see the beauty in, all because I have a deeper understanding of the design process. For Eddy, he has learned about colour and warmth and that amazing pieces of designer furniture are not enough to make a home – you need emotion and soul and a very good sense of space and colour. Otherwise it's just a showroom.

How do you incorporate colour into your home?

Colour is in our home in so many ways. To begin with, I am unafraid of paint. It is the easiest and cheapest way to bring not only colour, but your own inimitable style into your home. I play with paint a lot. I'm not afraid to mix my own, although I learned the hard way that you must make notes on what you have mixed in case you run out before the end of the job!

Then there are artworks, soft furnishings, rugs, vases – if you love and want colour around you there are a million ways to do it. We have brought colour in with all of these.

Having said all of this, I never made a clear decision to have lots of colour in the home, it has just evolved that way.

I love what yellow brings to this house. What a glorious colour it is. It's not the easiest necessarily to incorporate, but so rich and wonderful when you can.

Do you have a favourite item at home?

I am sentimental, so my favourite items usually have a personal story. The paintings by Louise Olsen and Stephen Ormandy would be among my favourite items. I love some of the furniture we have. The nature of our business means that things change, though. We keep them for a while, then let them go so they can find a worthy home elsewhere. Eddy loves rarity and the hunt. There are very few things he wouldn't change if something else caught his fancy. It's about the history and the provenance – once he has felt that, he can let go and move onto the next thing. I guess we both have current favourites.

How does colour influence the way you live?

I would say that it enhances rather than influences. It can soothe me, inspire me, bring me joy. If I feel stuck, I can create change with colour, either in the home, the garden or the wardrobe. The world offers us such an incredible palette to be inspired by, from the chaotically joyous and alive colours of Africa and India, to the beautifully stark whites and ice blues of the Arctic. I try to stay away from colour trends and stick with instinct and emotion.

Who or what inspires you?

Nature – light, colours, shapes and the sense of awe that nature offers us. Also my friends – I have wonderfully clever and creative friends.

And Italy; my god, I'm inspired by Italy.

For Eddy, it would be designers such as Afra and Tobia Scarpa or Osvaldo Borsani. Eddy lives and breathes furniture, so is always researching. If you have a curious mind, inspiration is everywhere really.

Do you have a favourite location or place to visit and why?

For both of us it is Italy. We just love it: the language, people, landscape, architecture, history, the designers.

My other favourite location is home. I am a profound homebody. For me, a good home means that once I am inside, the outside world ceases to exist. Encased in beauty and comfort. Many people confuse beauty and comfort with luxury. We can't all afford luxury, but if we want to, we can create beauty and comfort that makes our hearts sing.

STATE OF THE ART

Art has been a lifelong passion for me. Even from a preschool age, my mother recalls our shopping trips, where I would point out all the 'pretty pictures'. Later in life, galleries and exhibitions captivated me like little else could.

As adulthood approached, I was offered the choice between a party or cash to acknowledge this milestone. I knew exactly what I wanted: I chose the money – and bought my first piece of 'real' art: a limited-edition print by Charles Blackman from his *Alice in Wonderland* series. At the time I had no idea who Blackman was; it was a purchase straight from the heart and I am still smitten by its beauty many years later.

Of course, art can also be unattributed and bought for a bargain. Another of the most treasured pieces in my collection – a tapestry, significantly aged but with character in spades – was picked up at a Moroccan flea market for five dollars.

And my collection of shuttlecocks and shells, housed in vintage glassware, is just as important to me as the Blackman because of the memories and stories behind these items.

My point here is that the allure of art is completely subjective, and it can come in many forms. Quite simply, if you love it, the cost and who created it shouldn't matter.

However, there are a few tips you can apply when selecting and displaying your art, to make sure you get the most out of these treasured items.

1 – CHOOSING YOUR ART

The art world is filled with heavenly choice, from top-end auction items to affordable ready-to-hang works. From online marketplaces and antique shops to local studios and garage sales, artwork comes in every shape, size, style and form.

Usually, when we think of art, we think of a painting or a print, framed and displayed on a wall. But it can just as easily take the form of a sculpture, canvas, macramé, children's paintings or even a display of books.

In addition to the more traditional art forms, my own collection of artworks includes paintings created on circular plywood, handmade wooden totems, ceramics and even my collection of design books.

Aside from galleries, fabulous pieces can be found at flea markets, vintage poster stores, gift stores and via creative hubs such as Etsy.

The rule of thumb here is that if it speaks to you, it is meant to be yours.

2 – CREATING A COHESIVE SPACE

It is always important to consider the palette of the entire room and how your art combines with other decor pieces.

In my home, I have been known to allow the art to dictate other decorative decisions in a room – it may have been the first item I bought and everything else will fall into place alongside it.

The key here is to choose one colour from within the body of the artwork and reference it through soft furnishings or other decorative objects. This will make the overall space feel connected and considered.

3 – PRESENTING YOUR ART

When it comes to traditional artworks, how each piece is framed is a consideration that can make or break the look you are trying to achieve.

For prints, float framing is one of my favourite methods. This sees works set back – adhered to the back of the frame, which creates the appearance of floating within the frame itself. Simple blonde wood frames are an effective way to set off the work without taking away from it, but this is a matter of personal taste: a white or black frame may suit the wall better. The style of artwork can also dictate your choice of frame, and it's important to match these consistently. Sometimes, a more ornate style will work best and create an elegant effect.

When framing your art behind glass, a mount board can provide a visual break between the image and the frame and works to draw the eye towards the art. If customised, they can add a shot of complimentary colour too.

A shadow box frame, which has a fixed space between the glass and the artwork to create a three-dimensional effect, also looks finished and considered.

4 – COMPOSITION AND SCALE

It's important to consider the size of the piece in relation to the area it's displayed in. For maximum impact, make sure you think about the scale of your artwork on its wall or shelf. A small artwork will be consumed by space on a large wall, so opt for a large piece of art – it's worth the investment. Similarly, a smaller artwork lends itself to a shelf vignette and might be your opportunity to add an original piece by your favourite artist to your collection.

If you are lucky enough to have your own collections, grouping artworks together to create a gallery effect can work well. In this instance, composition is as important as the work itself. A salon hang sees pieces grouped in a jigsaw configuration and is an effective way of displaying treasured items together.

5 – HANGING YOUR ART

Hanging art can be quite a science and one that can go wrong if rushed. It's important to do your research, particularly when it comes to hanging heavy pieces, as a matter of both safety and aesthetics.

Before you take hammer and nail to the wall, I suggest measuring your art and using masking tape to mimic the shape and size of the pieces in position on the wall. You don't want to be banging more holes in walls than is necessary, so take the guesswork out of it and create a spatial preview to ensure it looks right.

If you rent your home and are unable to hammer nails into your walls, try using adhesive hooks from hardware stores – they don't mark the walls.

You can also clip your unframed artwork, tape it, place it under a glass dome or invest in high-tech gallery hanging systems.

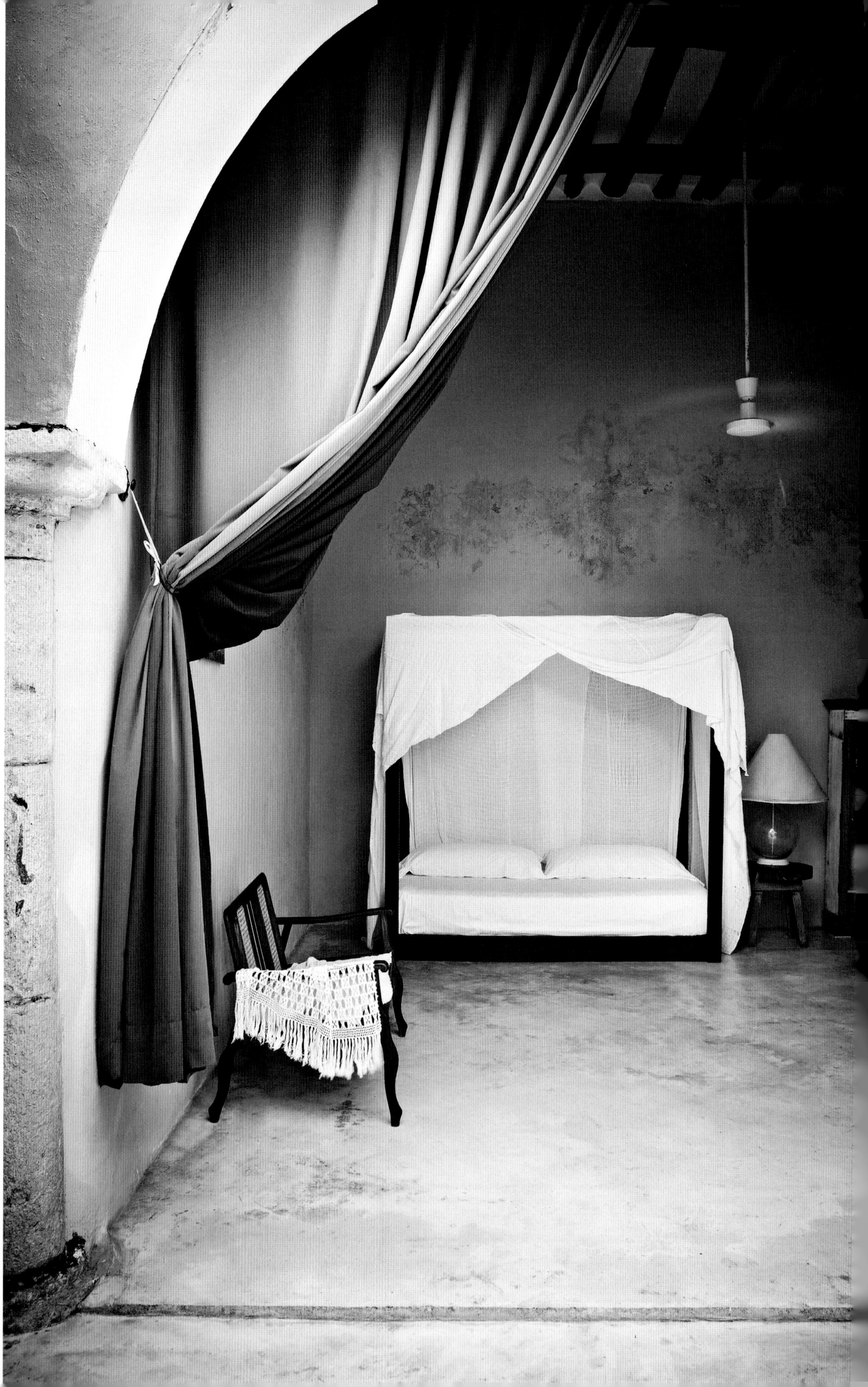

I am not known as someone who embraces a lot of white or neutrals, but putting my own colour preferences aside, I know there are others who feel more comfortable – physically and emotionally – in spaces that are minimal and less coloured.

Every interior needs to be balanced and have a place where people can rest their eyes without feeling visually worn out. Rooms that embrace a natural palette can be calm spaces that offer quiet and contemplation. A place to let your imagination run wild, or just be still.

In addition, some spaces call for understated interiors based on their relationship to the surrounding geography. A well-known example is a coastal look for a beachside house.

Typically speaking, the coastal look boasts cool, crisp and calm white interior spaces, so as to enhance the view or even magnify the blue of the ocean. This deliberate use of a neutral palette works well and is a powerful tool when it comes to interior styling.

White and grey are tones widely used – together and separately. The range of shades and tints is broad. I like to call them Switzerland colours: harmonious at all times and avowedly neutral. They will always be on trend.

The beauty of a natural palette is that it works in every room in the house. Kitchens and bathrooms are the obvious choices when it comes to working with a lighter palette, with cabinetry, benchtops and tiling all suited to a snowy colour scheme. My tip here is to incorporate timber or metallic decor or hardware to add interest and warmth.

In bedrooms and living areas, it's all about texture. In my experience, geolocation homes that successfully embrace neutrals – think powder, nude, taupe, oatmeal and stone – are most effective when this colour scheme is executed using different materials. Texture really matters when there is little differentiation in the shades, and it is critical to add depth, soul and warmth to a space.

Go for accessories such as linen cushions or bedding, chunky knit throws, plush woven rugs and even seating in a luxe velvet or faux shearling to create textural warmth. This can then be complemented by indoor greenery, which also adds a textural element, as well as colour and life – both important features in avoiding that dreaded feeling of sterility.

Oh, and don't be fooled into thinking that choosing the 'right' white for an interior is an easy task – it is a science. Pale walls bounce light around like nobody's business, so the way the two interact is most important.

↑ White – all its many commercial shades – is a changeable colour, absorbing other hues and displaying differently in relation to the amount of surrounding light (or lack thereof). To avoid it feeling like a science lab, inject colour onto the walls with art and decorative objects, or via fabrics and furniture. Go as bold as you like for maximum contrast.

→ Scale can make or break a room. Larger rooms can take a few larger pieces, layered with smaller items. Remember that a variety of sizes is more visually pleasing than uniform or many too-small items. Personalise the space with one or two oversized three-dimensional decorator items.

Rustic spaces love a white carcass to show off their character and often their age – liming or whitewashing homes is centuries old. White walls and ceilings can make for fresh and interesting interiors if they are layered with time-worn pieces, natural materials and the warmth of wood. Try configuring your all-white space using some of these principles.

← Light white and bright spaces work well if decorated in either a minimalist or maximalist way. A must with all-white interiors is to mix materials and show signs of life – this is what elevates it from vacuous to meaningful. And always play with texture to add body and dimension to the space.

← Mixed materiality is what makes this minimalist monochrome lounge so striking. Sometimes less is genuinely better: it's about editing, rather than adding. This is one of the most important design principles of styling. Start with bare floors and walls and add one piece at a time until the composition feels right to you.

Anything structural in a space, such as beams, can be quite an obstacle to the flow of the room. White ensures the beams remain a feature but blend into the space better than if they were left a solid colour.

Veined white marble is an opulent look, not just reserved for the wet rooms of the house. If your budget does not extend to an entire bathroom fit-out in marble, consider a marble entry – a smaller and less traditional space for luxury stone, but a light and cool arrival point nonetheless.

A monochrome palette will never date. Ever. Black steel window inserts/trims break up an all-white space and are strong bones for a contemporary style. To avoid clutter and continue with the minimalist theme, consider track lighting in spaces such as this for a gallery-type feel within the home.

Maintaining a minimal white interior means restraint. Add layers, without overcomplicating things, by using glass, whether that be in your decorator choices or your table lighting. That way the space continues to flow, uninterrupted.

Martyn Thompson

Sydney, Australia

Tell us a little about creating this space. What was it inspired by?

This is the house of my wonderful late friend, Penny Galwey. I have been living here since the pandemic lockdown when I came back to Sydney. Penny and I shared a passion for interiors. She was my chief adviser whenever I was working on a new collection or an installation. I'm living in her old bedroom which I have 'Martynified' with a wall of the handpainted plates that I make with British ceramic company 1882 Ltd.

Have you always loved colour?

In my early twenties, when I made clothes commercially, I used tapestry fabrics and patchworked colourful jersey. I've always been attracted to colour. As a photographer, I tend towards a recognisable colour palette.

How has your style evolved over the years?

I like a lot of the same things. The difference now is that I am more conscious of what they are. I was always attracted to the artist's house. In the '80s I was mad about painted wooden furniture (as were many other people) and I still love this today. In the '90s I was introduced to mid-century design and that has become a part of my aesthetic. I've worked with a handful of amazing designers and artists, each of whom left their mark: Ilse Crawford, Vincent Van Duysen, Elsa Peretti.

Do you have a favourite colour, pattern or similar that you often turn to?

There is a certain tonality that I love; a mid-tone that creates the perfect background for me. I'm not a fan of white walls.

How do you incorporate colour into your home?

Everywhere! I always use colour on the walls. Painted shades of green greys, dusky pinks and earthy beige.

Or I use fabrics on the wall, my jacquards. My palette isn't bright but it is full of colour. I like warm highlights of yellows, reds or oranges among the cool and neutral tones – the blues, browns and greys. Pink is a current favourite accent.

Different colours look good in different places and in different types of light, so I need to consider where an interior is based. Is there a predominance of daylight or is the lighting all artificial? That makes such a difference to how colour reads. What looks good in New York doesn't necessarily look good in Sydney.

Do you have a favourite item at home?

Items plural: what I sleep in and what I eat from. This is important to me. Bed linen is quite an obsession. I have a variety and mix them together, mood dependent. Tea pots, cups, plates and cutlery; combining patterns and colours: making these small choices is pleasing. Also – some blatant self promotion – I love the jacquard textile that I make. It has such a depth to it. Everything I have is upholstered in it, my walls are patchwork covered in it.

How does colour influence the way you live?

Colour is mood. I seek emotional tranquillity and colour is key to creating this.

Who or what inspires you?

Light inspires me. When I am looking for somewhere to live or somewhere to work, my first consideration is the natural light. The quality of light is essential to how I feel. I don't like dark spaces or bright artificial light.

Do you have a favourite location or place to visit and why?

The daunting and inspiring landscapes of Iceland. Their aquatic centres with multiple pools and thermal spas, and most of all their general elven queerness.

SHELVES

One of the things I am asked remarkably often is how to create beautifully styled shelves. That's because, as anyone who has ever tried to create the perfect shelf display knows, even the simplest arrangement can take a surprising amount of tweaking and reshuffling to get it looking just right.

Long before web meetings prompted people to style – or at least organise – their on-screen backgrounds, a considered shelf of interesting and beautiful things has been a magnet in a home.

And it's easy to understand why – not only is it an opportunity to create visual interest in your home, it's also a chance to put some of your most prized possessions on display. After all, these are the pieces that tell stories and spark memories – a well-styled shelf can inject a huge amount of personality into a home. It's also a chance to bring in beautiful bursts of colour that catch the eye and connect with other objects in the room, creating a unified space.

It's not an exact science, but composition plays the most important role when styling shelves. Ideally, they should create a journey for the eye, with height and scale your primary guides. Whether you want a minimalist and uncluttered display or shelves that are generously laden with trinkets – both can make a big impact – the placement of your objects should always take height and scale into consideration. For an interesting composition, your shelf should contain a mix of objects of different heights that follow the line of a bell curve.

Naturally, books are a fabulous item to include on any shelf display. Book spines can not only infuse personality into a space by offering clues about their owner, but they are a wonderful way to introduce colour to a space.

Book covers come in all the colours of the rainbow, and with a little organising of your collection, you can use books as stylistic elements – accentuating those that are of the same shade as other items in your room is a clever option for subtly unifying your space.

For a bolder shelf display that has maximum impact, consider colour coding your book spines; grouping similarly toned books together produces a dramatic effect. If you don't own a rainbow book collection diverse enough to pull this off, second-hand stores are worth scoping out. Likewise, removing old dust covers can reveal a new look on a hardback.

It can work to play around with the placement of the spines too, laying some blocks of books flat, and others upright. This is an effective way to create interest and encourage curiosity, which is what your shelf should be all about.

While you're scouring the charity shops and market stalls, keep an eye out for tinted glass vessels, vases and bottles. The same way colour groupings of books make a playful statement, glass objects grouped in similar hues make for a fabulous display. You can mix modern pieces with traditional brilliant cut glass, with colour being their theme. Glassware is readily found in a whole range

of shades, including amber, green, blue, pink and plum, and you can have fun both in the search and the informal final result.

Another fail-safe option for any shelf is greenery. The beautiful foliage of house plants works wonders in brightening up any display and instantly adds life to a shelf.

My go-to plant choices are hanging varieties such as chain of hearts, devil's ivy, or even mother-in-law's tongue for its graphic shape. All hardy varieties, they are well suited to shelf life and can also provide an important vertical element. Remember, too, that indoor plants are not limited to just shades of green – they can be speckled, striped or veined, with white, yellow, pink and deep-red toned foliage all readily available. These variegated and coloured leaf types might be just the thing for your shelf.

Ceramics, sculptures and art can also star on any shelf, and the combination of objects is purely at the discretion of the person creating it. While a randomised approach can still make a genuinely interesting display, consider some repetition for a more polished look. Look for hints of colour that pick up on similar themes in your display to create connectivity and consistency. And if a certain curio has significance, consider giving it its own shelf, or put a glass dome over the object to signify its special nature.

Placement of the shelves can be just as important as what you put on them. Think of clever ways to use idle spaces: an otherwise unused corner can be repurposed with a shelving display. A shelf ledge above a bed can be

as practical as it is visually appealing, as it keeps the floor space clear of bedside tables, while doubling up as a space to lean artwork, stash books and other bedside treasures.

A certain amount of care is required with the installation of overhead shelves, so do be sure to think about position and the impact of toppling pieces before committing.

Your shelving display is really only limited by your imagination. But whether you are creating a setting that is bold or minimalist, multilayered or a single shelf, the most important thing to do is experiment. Trial and error is an important step in getting it right. My tip is to take photos as you go – viewing them on screen away from the room somehow allows you to gauge its success more objectively. Building up a small photo library of your variations also lets you look back on what worked and what didn't.

I also recommend when you nail the look, don't leave it that way for years as a dusty collection you no longer even see. Refresh the display either partially or entirely every year or so. The renewal is worthwhile.

Shelves take work, so patience is paramount – but it is worth the effort.

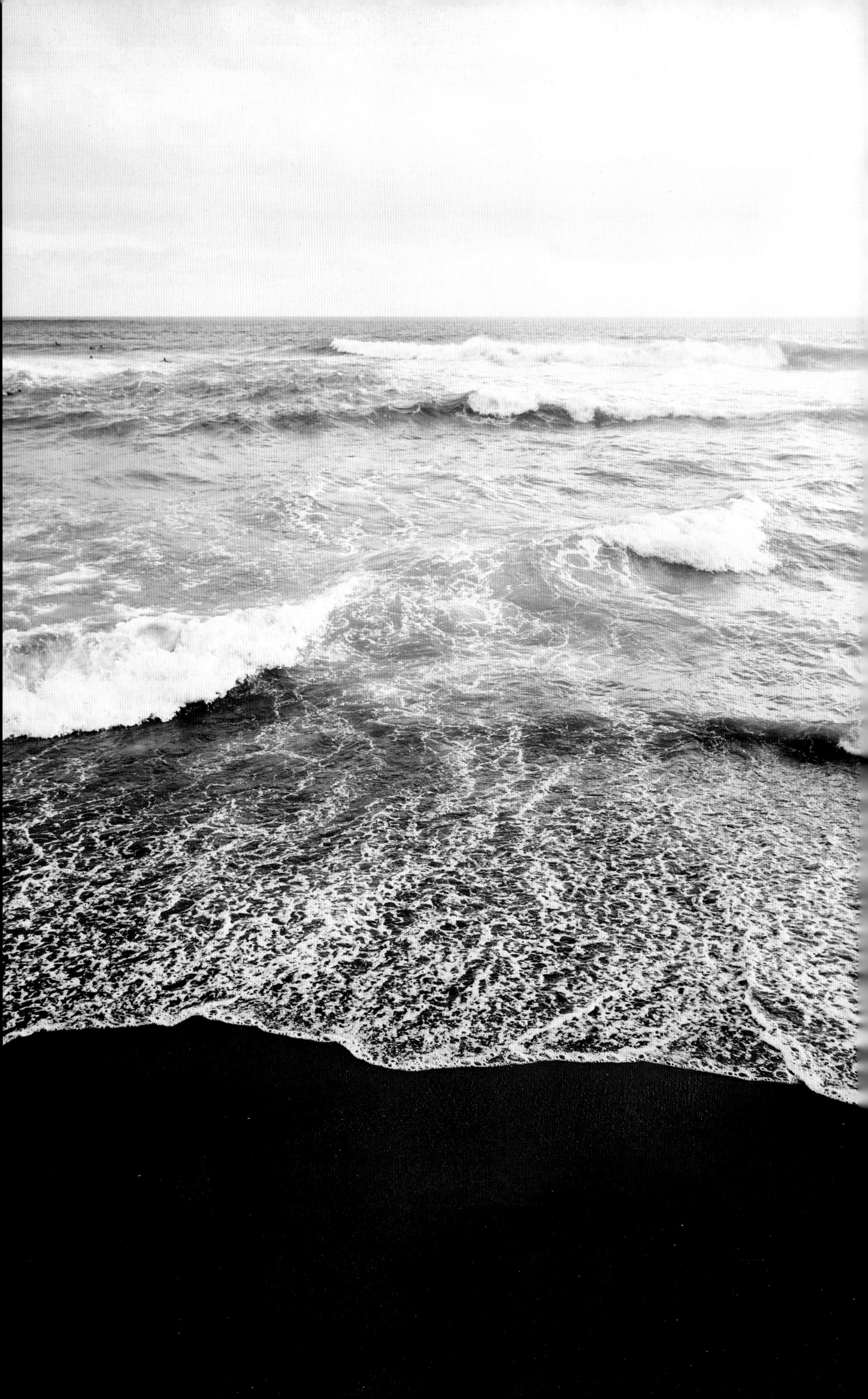

Black, off-black, charcoal and every moonless shade between are strong choices to use in the home, but boy, do they have a place. Black anchors a space, adding a crispness and definition to large and small areas. It excels as a dignified counterpoint.

The absence of colour in black is what highlights depth and variation in all other hues – simply put, black can make all other colours come alive. It is the ultimate foil in interiors while still delivering on the mood.

In colour theory, black represents strength and sophistication, and it's hugely popular in many design fields, including fashion. Translated to interiors, it is stimulating and elegant and – just like the best wardrobe staple – it goes with everything.

Moderate how much black (and its spectrum) goes into an interior space so as not to overwhelm, but black does work in every room in the house.

Living room needs a lift? No problem – black can immediately transform your space from dull to dramatic. When paired with contrasting white walls and skirting boards, a deep charcoal feature wall can provide depth or is the perfect backdrop for a gallery wall.

Kitchens, too, lend themselves to a sleek, dark hue. Onyx cabinetry and appliances add elegance in a modern space or create a feeling of intimacy in a more traditional interior.

You may like to experiment with the smallest room in the house first. Bathrooms, second bathrooms or powder rooms are well suited to black – patterned tiles, wallpaper, tapware and cabinetry are all excellent choices for introducing ebony tones into bathrooms, especially when paired with a contrasting, lighter colour.

If paint or fixed furnishings are too much of an outlay, a chic, sophisticated look can be achieved through dark-to-black furniture and homewares. Try using larger pieces such as a sofa or sideboard, or smaller accessories such as lamps, mirrors and frames in a considered repetition of black to unify your space.

Far from a mere modern declaration of cool, black has timeless appeal and it works with almost any style of home: traditional to contemporary, coastal to boho.

← Rather than flat black walls, consider textured panelling or even corrugated iron for increased effect and depth. Counter the strength of this with warm and woolly textures in neutral tones. The weathered look of leather and wood integrates well too.

← Black is unparalleled when it comes to adding drama to a space.
With sufficient natural light and contrasting decor in the space to
balance it, black really is just as versatile and safe an option as white.

The bold nature of black can be used to great effect when paired with bolts of equally intense colour. Inject bright accents alongside this dark hue and watch its personality transform from moody to punchy. Include gold for extra glamour.

Another excellent way to add life and light into a black interior is with the clever use of mirrors that reflect a lighter colour – in this instance white. This optical illusion can illuminate the space without the use of any artificial lighting.

Don't be afraid to go to the dark side. Consider how much black to incorporate into your interior, alongside its materiality. Glossy black accents can create immediate glamour, while time-worn black leather can point to comfort. To avoid a cave-like effect, introduce other bold colours, mirrors or a white ceiling.

→ Architectural details of homes – doorways, arches, shutters, panelling, frames and trims – are transformed using black or charcoal. Essentially, these are all black frames, assuredly defining an object or a view; be sure to balance the effect with textured and contrasting decor.

Black is a great mixer, tying decor pieces from different periods together, even those of different styles. Despite the obvious contrasting influences, the consistent use of black consolidates a space.

Daiji Takai and Yasuko Takai

Kyoto, Japan

Tell us a little about creating this space. What was it inspired by?
We try to own only the furniture we need. Most of the items in our long, narrow house were given to us by acquaintances, so the interior is entirely composed of those 'accidental gatherings'.

Have you always loved colour?
I particularly like natural shades and we love black and white.

How has your style evolved over the years?
I used to like '60s Scandinavian design, but as I have become older I have become more attracted to naturalistic and simple things. Our style in the house has remained almost unchanged; we have just added a few books and CDs that we liked over time.

Do you have a favourite colour, pattern or similar that you often turn to?
I'm drawn to the design and colours of African Kuba cloth. The patterns are generous and powerful.

How do you incorporate colour into your home?
We have an even distribution of two shades that happen to be at the extremes of the colour spectrum: black and white. We supplement these hues with touches of colour through the use of plants, flowers and pottery.

Do you have a favourite item at home?
Our bookshelf is filled with the rich colours of old books. An old book is imbued with history – the times and events that it has experienced. Old books anchor people, linking past and present; they tell us where we are now.

How does colour influence the way you live?
We live surrounded by natural colours and are deeply moved by the delicate shades of plants and fruits when the seasons change. Colour soothes the mind and refreshes.

Do you have a favourite location or place to visit and why?
We often go to Kamo River in Kyoto. Watching the slow flow of water is very calming.

SMALL SPACES

Whether it's an environmentally conscious decision, a tiny rented space or a first foray into the real estate market, most of us have lived in a small house at one time in our lives; many still do.

There is no doubt that smaller homes present their own challenges, from storage issues to avoiding clutter. But I am here to tell you that regardless of your compact floorplan, small homes can feel roomy and be every bit as stylish as a more expansive abode.

There is no reason why you can't wave your colour-loving wand in any space, regardless of its size – it is all about being considered with your choices. Small spaces do require thought, but by following a few savvy styling tricks, your home will feel less like a tiny shoebox and more spacious and free-flowing.

CONSIDER EVERY ITEM
This is true of every space but critical when it comes to decorating a smaller home – only keep what you need. If you use it, keep it. Ditch it if you don't.

I've never seen a small house that had more storage than it needed, so by culling those superfluous pieces you'll eliminate the clutter and allow your remaining items space to breathe, and subsequently add to the feeling of openness.

Care with colour is especially vital when working in small areas – too much can overpower and enclose a space; just one major element or a handful of carefully chosen pieces may be enough.

USE PAINT TO ADVANTAGE
One of the easiest ways to open up any space is with paint. Your colour choice can have a major impact on making a space feel more open than it is. Light-coloured paint on the walls is an understandable choice as it will make any space feel bright and spacious, but if you are feeling a tad more daring, there are other palettes that can also give a small room a big boost.

Blush tones, for example, have a warm glow and light reflects beautifully off them, adding to the feeling of spaciousness. Moody tones, counterintuitively, can make a room feel more expansive than it actually is. A darker room paired with light furniture can create an optical illusion, making the space feel larger.

Painting the walls and ceiling in the same shade, whether dark or light, can also deceive the eye by disguising where corner lines start and stop. It's a simple solution for any room that feels small.

But don't be confined to paint only to get your colour fix. Play with tiles – wall and floor – and paint for a dramatic and colourful look in small spaces.

PLAY WITH SCALE
A smaller space needs smaller decor, right? Not necessarily. Bigger is actually better with some items. A larger rug, for example, has the effect of drawing the eye out, creating the impression of a larger space. So that fabulously hued tribal rug that you've been admiring might fit the brief.

Floor tiles work in the same way and are another great way to introduce a pop of colour into a smaller room. The strategic use of scale creates an optical illusion that can be used to advantage and works just as well with bold tones as it does with neutrals. I have used highly patterned green Moroccan encaustic tiles and moody black walls to great effect in a powder room, making the floor space feel bigger, yet cocooned by the dark walls.

LOOK FOR CREATIVE STORAGE SOLUTIONS
Look for ways to create more storage by making use of otherwise empty spaces. Trundles or boxes on wheels are ideal for under a bed, or look to add extra shelves in existing cupboards to increase your useable space.

MAKE USE OF DEAD SPACE
Real estate is at a premium in smaller houses, so innovative options for unused spaces can be a game changer. Look critically at every area in your home, including vertical spaces and voids, as a potential location. A dead corner can easily be transformed into a useable space with a compact table or some floating shelving – turning an otherwise redundant space into a neat work area or a place to display some decorative objects.

CREATE AIRFLOW
The largest pieces in your house – key furniture items – need not feel big and bulky. Again, it's all smoke and mirrors to create that optical illusion. The secret here is to go for pieces that allow for airflow: a sofa on legs will look and feel less bulky than one that goes right to the floor.

Your home should be as functional and appealing as it can possibly be, regardless of its size. Spend some time assessing your small space, and size up its potential as an ideal starter project for colour and creativity.

Credits

Cover: Home of Eryca Green and Eddy Opmanis

Front endpaper: Frida's house, Mexico City, Mexico

Pages 2, 10, 14–26, 29, 31: Rozemarijn de Witte and Pierre Traversier | www.losenamoradosibiza.com

Pages 4, 182–6, 188–93, 195 (right), 196–7: Eryca Green and Eddy Opmanis | www.smithstreetbazaar.com | Styling by Julia Green

Page 6: Gallaratese – Monte Amiata © Derek Swalwell

Pages 6, 109–14, 144–5, 155, 195 (left): home of Heather Nette King | www.heathernetteking.com.au

Pages 8, 49, 120, 180, 181: Havana, Cuba

Pages 32, 99, 220: Dubrovnik, Croatia

Page 36: Jenny and Peter Nyary | www.nyary.com.au | Story and styling by Heather Nette King | Published by Fairfax Media

Pages 38–43, 50–1, 233 (right): Kylie and Andrew O'Toole | Design by www.residentavenue.com.au | Styling by Julia Green

Pages 44–5, 83, 115, 162–4, 165 (left), 167: Gavin Brown | www.gavinbrown.com.au | Styling by Vicky Valsamis

Pages 46–7, 63, 70–3: Roger Ward | roger.thorntonward@bigpond.com | Styling by Heather Nette King

Page 48: Las Vegas, USA

Pages 52–4, 57–61: Eddie and Dorothy Spain | Design by Resident Avenue www.residentavenue.com.au | Styling by Heather Nette King

Page 64: Sicily, Italy

Pages 68–9: Budapest, Hungary

Pages 74–5, 77–8, 82, 123, 208: Clare Littlewood | clare.littlewood@libero.it | Styling by Mariella Ienna

Page 76: Filicudi, Italy

Page 79: Simon Digby | Designed by Resident Avenue www.residentavenue.com.au | Styling by Sami Johnson

Page 80: Trinidad, Cuba

Pages 81, 117, 138, 244: Marrakech, Morocco

Pages 84, 121, 169, 211: Hoshinoya Kyoto | www.hoshinoresorts.com

Pages 85, 100, 122, 124–6, 128–9, 176–8: El Fenn | www.el-fenn.com

Pages 86–90, 217–19: Mariella Ienna | mariella.ienna.design@gmail.com

Page 93: NYC, USA

Pages 94, 104: Le Jardin, Marrakech, Morocco

Pages 98, 140–1: Alice and Gaby Paris | www.riad-yasmine.com

Pages 101–2, 105, 198: Ariane Dutzi | www.dutzishop.com

Pages 106–7: The Bank Studio | www.thebankstudio.com

Page 108: Georgie Wilson | www.georgiewilson.com.au

Page 116: Hondarribia, Spain

Page 118: www.riadjardinsecret.com

Pages 119, 160: Sam Scully | www.theflatironlabel.com.au | Story and styling by Heather Nette King | Published by Fairfax Media

Page 131: Naoshima Island, Japan

Pages 132, 156: www.berberlodge.net

Pages 136–7: Michael Artemenko | www.figr.com.au | Art by Kate Ballis | Styling by Julia Green | Published in Are Media.

Pages 139, 142: Venice, Italy

Page 143: Valladolid, Mexico

Pages 146–53: Laurence Leenaert | www.lrnce.com

Page 155: Screenprint © Bonnie and Neil

Page 161: Guy Mathews | www.guymathewsindustrial.com | Story and styling by Heather Nette King | Published by Fairfax Media

Pages 165 (right), 166: Gavin Brown | www.gavinbrown.com.au | Story and styling by Heather Nette King | Published by Fairfax Media

Pages 168, 221, 240, 262: designed by Roger Ward | roger.thorntonward@bigpond.com

Pages 170–3: *Reversible Destiny Lofts Mitaka – In Memory of Helen Keller*, created in 2005 by Arakawa and Madeline Gins © 2005 Estate of Madeline Gins | www.rdloftsmitaka.com

Page 174: Sarah Fletcher | www.fletcherarts.com | Story and styling by Heather Nette King | Published by Fairfax Media

Page 175: Georgia Danos | www.gracemelbourne.com.au | Story and styling by Heather Nette King | Published by Fairfax Media

Page 202: San Sebastian, Spain

Pages 204–6, 246–7: John Henry | www.johnhenryarchitects.com.au

Pages 207, 233 (left), 239, 242–3: Shauna Toohey and Misha Hollenbach | www.perksandmini.com | Styling by Vicky Valsamis

Page 209: Sicily, Italy

Pages 210, 254–6, 259: Daiji Takai and Yasuko Takai | www.mustard-3rd.com

Pages 212–15: www.setouchi-aonagi.com

Pages 216, 238: www.oblica.com.au | Art by Aylsa McHugh | Styling by Julia Green

Pages 222–5 | www.conradarchitects.com | Story and styling by Heather Nette King | Published by Fairfax Media

Pages 226–8, 230–1: Martyn Thompson | www.martynthompson.com | Styling by Julia Green

Page 234: Uluwatu, Bali, Indonesia

Page 241: Zlarin Island, Croatia

Pages 248–51: Kali Cavanagh | www.kalicavanagh.com | Styling by Julia Green

Page 252: Stuart Mckenzie | www.southofjohnston.com.au | Published by Murdoch | Styling by Deborah Kaloper

Page 262: Sculpture © Kate Rhode

Back endpaper: Mexico City, Mexico

Julia Green

It had always been a dream to create a book, but not one I ever really thought would happen.

And it wouldn't have if it weren't for my supportive family, allowing me to be everywhere but home, chasing down beautiful interior spaces to style and write about. Adam Green, you are my rock of thirty-one years and the most beautiful father on the planet, so I know our kids have not missed out on a thing with you by their side. Thank you for being so solid, always, and to my kids for their big bear hugs every time I come home.

I have to thank my mother for injecting her love of colour into my veins from an early age. I know it's your influence and passion that has brought me to where I am today. Thanks Jillima.

I am still pinching myself that Hardie Grant so graciously embraced our idea for this book on colour. Jane and Anna, you are amazing humans, and your support and guidance has been a total blessing. Thanks not only for your faith, but for getting Daniel onto the design team – his work on the book has brought the vision to life. Thanks also to editor Kate Daniel, and to my friend Suzie Coffey for being my sounding board on all things word-related.

The biggest thanks of all goes to the new and old colour-loving friends we have met and featured along the way; what an honour to share time with you all and to witness your creative genius at play. It is truly a privilege to be invited into your homes, and one I am eternally grateful for.

Armelle, my co-author and work spouse – we did it! Professionally, I look up to you more than any other. You have taught me almost everything I know, and I am indebted to you for that, but also very lucky to call you one of my best friends. Going to 'work' with you is never really work, but a total joy.

Thanks in advance to those who buy this book, we hope you love it!

Long live colour!

Armelle Habib

This book has been a long time coming, and is like a visual diary of my last decade, travelling the world and capturing moments. I could not have done this without the support of my partner, Bruno, who has held the fort at home, brilliantly parenting our five-year-old, Wilfred. Thank you to both of you for allowing me to do what I love best, next to spending time with you! I am a better person with a camera around my neck, and you both know it.

It's an honour and privilege to be allowed into people's homes, their private sanctuaries, and one I never take for granted. Thank you to all of the creatives that have permitted me the time to photograph them; I am grateful for this and humbled by it also.

Creating a book takes a tribe. First and foremost, I wish to thank Hardie Grant for the opportunity and for believing in my work. Jane and Anna, your shared vision and excitement for this book has been a blessing. I would also like to acknowledge Daniel for his design work and for making this book shine. We are so fortunate to have worked with you.

Finally, thanks to the stylists that have collaborated with me, in particular my mate and co-author, Julia Green, who not only shares my love for colour but trusts me implicitly. It's not every day you get to make your dream book with one of your best mates. It sure has been one hell of a wild ride, full of unforgettable moments, all treasured.

Armelle Habib

Armelle Habib is one of Australia's leading lifestyle photographers, with an international portfolio covering interiors, food, travel and lifestyle. Her work is featured in many notable magazines and books, such as *Elle Deco* (UK), *Living etc* (UK), *IDEAT* (France), *Vogue Living* and *Belle*. She regularly contributes to *Inside Out*, *House & Garden*, *Home Beautiful* and *Sunday Life* magazines.

Armelle has also collaborated on many cookbooks for Hardie Grant, Plum and Murdoch, and has an expansive commercial portfolio of advertising clients, designers and architects.

Armelle is known best for her love of natural light, as well as for capturing moments in time that are captivating and candid. When she is not travelling, Armelle resides in Melbourne, Australia.

Julia Green

Julia Green is an interior stylist and writer known best for her love of colour. Her work has been featured widely in both Australian and European publications, and she is a regular contributor to *Inside Out*, *Home Beautiful* and *House & Garden* magazines.

Julia has been an authoritative voice in the interiors arena for years, co-hosting the Channel 10 series *The Home Team* as the interiors expert and appearing as a guest speaker on *Grand Designs*, at Life Instyle and for the Porter Davis home series. She was recently appointed as the Dulux Australia Colour Ambassador.

Julia has a wide and varied commercial styling portfolio of advertising clients, designers and architects. When she is not styling, she is mentoring and promoting a select group of artists and makers for her own branded agency, Greenhouse Interiors.

Julia lives by the beach, in Barwon Heads, Victoria, and wishes she could see more of it. However, styling and colour are her passion, so she continues to chase down rainbows.

Published in 2021 by Hardie Grant Books,
an imprint of Hardie Grant Publishing

Hardie Grant Books (Melbourne)
Wurundjeri Country
Building 1, 658 Church Street
Richmond, Victoria 3121

Hardie Grant Books (London)
5th & 6th Floors
52–54 Southwark Street
London SE1 1UN

hardiegrantbooks.com

Hardie Grant acknowledges the Traditional Owners of the country on which we
work, the Wurundjeri people of the Kulin nation and the Gadigal people of the
Eora nation, and recognises their continuing connection to the land, waters and
culture. We pay our respects to their Elders past, present and emerging.

A catalogue record for this
book is available from the
National Library of Australia

Vivid
ISBN 9781 74379 650 4

10 9 8 7 6 5 4 3 2

Publishing Director: Jane Willson
Project Editor: Anna Collett
Editor: Kate Daniel
Design Manager: Mietta Yans
Designer: Daniel New
Photographer: Armelle Habib
Production Manager: Todd Rechner

Colour reproduction by Splitting Image Colour Studio
Printed in China by Leo Paper Products LTD.

The paper this book is printed on is from FSC®-certified forests and other sources.
FSC® promotes environmentally responsible, socially beneficial and economically
viable management of the world's forests.